An Indie Next pick

Advance Praise for rough house

"What is it like to be a refugee in your own country, to be a child in exile from safety, lost from landmarks again and again, waking each day to a search for some provisional sense of home? Tina Ontiveros takes us on that journey, where 'it's difficult to place memories in a childhood of migrations'— migrations from house to house season by season, from fury to joy in a moment, and from confusion to provisional certainties hard-won growing up. When W. H. Auden talks about a writer's 'clear expression of mixed feelings,' he could have been describing this book's power to put you inside the mind of a child beset by constant contradictions, her admiration and intermittent love for a parent beset by alcohol and given to destruction. In spite of her struggle, there is something so plucky and honest about this book's narrator, you will be converted to a new view of your own troubles. You will look at your own life through the lens of this book, knowing with Ontiveros that 'certain beauties can only be seen in the complication of hardship.' This kid's got the goods to survive, and this book's got a big story for you."

—Kim Stafford, author of *Singer Come from Afar*

"Set in the magnificent landscapes of Idaho, Oregon, Washington, and California, Tina Ontiveros's *rough house* portrays with empathy, insight, and humor the hardscrabble lives of a logging family broken by alcohol and constant displacement. Violence is a natural element of this rugged environment, but so is tenderness and fierce love. Besides Ontiveros herself, the memoir's central character is her complex father Loyd, whose difficulties and humanity electrify every page. Ontiveros's prose is intimate and unsentimental, eloquent testimony to life in hard times and the grit it takes to endure. *rough house* opens a window onto life in America far beyond the limits of Ontiveros's own family. Clearly, she is a writer working with deep reserves of talent, intelligence, and heart."

—DJ Lee, author of *Remote: Finding Home in the Bitterroots*

"Tina Ontiveros's *rough house* describes, with nuance, in lucid and always descriptive, swift prose, the ways poverty shapes family attachments and how the love attachment in particular is more mysterious and agitating than we can fathom. Ontiveros's portrayal of Loyd, the father character, is complex, empathetic, and truthful—emblematic of the way men become debilitated by masculine shame and loneliness. Midway through, the narrator says, 'I'm not sure the vocabulary exists to explain what that felt like.' Ontiveros presents a richly emotional and revelatory vocabulary for family in rural America."

—Jay Ponteri, author of *LOBE* and *Wedlocked*

"*rough house* is truly one of the best books I've read this year. Tina's story of growing up in trailers and logging camps throughout the Pacific Northwest is a tough, hard, sometimes horrifying read, but brilliant spots of love and joy throughout show that family is family is family. Family makes us who we are now and, regardless of where you grew up, or who grew you up, Tina's life story will surely resonate with every reader in one way or the other."

—Rene Kirkpatrick, University Bookstore (Seattle, Washington)

"*rough house* is at once a study of a disappearing culture, and an exotic and achingly familiar meditation on family. Amidst an unforgettable world of sawdust and grime, snarling chainsaws and privation, Ontiveros is as vivid in her in description as she is unflinching in her honesty."

—Jonathan Evison, author of *Lawn Boy* and *West of Here*

"The title of Tina Ontiveros's new memoir, *rough house*, says it all, describing both the delight of her clever father and his menacing flip-side. Ontiveros pulls no punches in portraying a hardscrabble childhood in Pacific Northwest logging camps and her desperate love for a darkly complicated man."

—Debra Gwartney, author of *I Am a Stranger Here Myself* and *Live Through This*

"*rough house* is a deeply realized memoir about family, addiction, violence, molestation, and the ways regular people endure and overcome inter-generational family dysfunction."

—Keenan Norris, author of *Brother and the Dancer* and *By the Lemon Tree*

"I read *rough house* in a single sitting, unable to break loose from the tension of what might happen next. It is the story of a childhood gone wrong in the wilds of the Pacific Northwest, twisted and tangled, before it is finally set to rights. Reminiscent of Raymond Carver if Carver had given a voice to the women and children faced with the troubles and misdeeds of men. From the myth of a larger-than-life father wracked with addiction and rage, to a steady and clear-eyed mother who remained at the center of her children's orbiting lives, *rough house* chronicles a past that haunts a young girl who, like her father, is filled with a legacy of anger, but like her mother, is determined to reshape how her own story will end."

—Deborah Reed, author of *Pale Morning Light With Violet Swan*, owner of Cloud & Leaf Bookstore (Manzanita, Oregon)

"Family, love, loss, peppered with a touch of 80s nostalgia makes this the perfect memoir. Find a spot under your favorite tree, breathe deep, then dive in."

—Sarah, Village Books (Bellingham, Washington)

"Ontiveros deftly invites us into her world and shares her story of rural living in this memoir of growing up in the timber industry. While I could relate to so much of her story, her window into the world of rural Oregon was illuminating and intriguing for this city girl. Ontiveros's masterful and sensitive style brings the characters to life and you can't help but love and despise them at the same time. A great read and a very real story. A must for anyone who calls the Pacific Northwest home."

—Kim Bissel, Broadway Books (Portland, Oregon)

Download reading group discussion questions at
http://osupress.oregonstate.edu/book/rough-house

rough house

rough house

tina ontiveros

a memoir

oregon state university press   corvallis

Library of Congress Cataloging-in-Publication Data

Names: Ontiveros, Tina, author.
Title: Rough house : a memoir / Tina Ontiveros.
Description: Corvallis, Oregon : Oregon State University Press, [2020]
Identifiers: LCCN 2020027183 (print) | LCCN 2020027184 (ebook) | ISBN
    9780870710339 (trade paperback) | ISBN 9780870710346 (ebook)
Subjects: LCSH: Ontiveros, Tina,—Family. | Working class women—
    Northwest, Pacific—Biography. | Loggers—Family relationships—Pacific
    Northwest. | Loggers—Pacific Northwest—Biography. | Fathers and
    daughters—Pacific Northwest—Biography. | Children of alcoholics—
    Pacific Northwest—Biography. | Children of divorced parents—Pacific
    Northwest—Biography. | Abusive men—Pacific Northwest—Biography. |
    Dysfunctional families—Pacific Northwest—Biography.
Classification: LCC CT275.O563 A3 2020 (print) | LCC CT275.O563
    (ebook) | DDC 979.092 [B]—dc23
LC record available at https://lccn.loc.gov/2020027183
LC ebook record available at https://lccn.loc.gov/2020027184

♾ This paper meets the requirements of ANSI/NISO Z39.48-1992
(Permanence of Paper).

First published in 2020 by Oregon State University Press
Fifth printing 2022
Printed in the United States of America

Oregon State University Press
121 The Valley Library
Corvallis OR 97331-4501
541-737-3166 • fax 541-737-3170
www.osupress.oregonstate.edu

for joan and jesse.
for linda, and for loyd.

contents

like riding a bike 1

timber child 7

something to cry about. 23

rough house 38

meetings 52

close call 70

steelhead 88

(the worst thing) 104

teen starter kit 115

high five 132

chalet café 149

other sheep 166

thank you 185

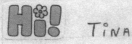 TINA   OCT. 1, 1981

        How's my Little
Sweetheart?

Daddy is Fine, and
Doing well.

Daddy Love's and misses
You and Jesse more
and more each Day.

And There's not a minute
of The day, That Daddy
Dose'nt Think of you Two.

So Please Don't ever Forget
Daddy.

Daddy Dase Care.

And Someday you and
Jesse will understan
That Daddy isn't really
Bad.

I Love you
Both very, very
    Much.

                        Daddy

like riding a bike

YOU MIGHT NOT CONSIDER my dad a good man. But if you'd met him, you probably would've liked him. Loyd was funny, slapstick even. Creative and industrious. He was always building or tinkering or exploring. He loved nature and magic, and, most of all, his children. But Loyd was never able to take good care of what he loved.

He made things that were so wholly his own, so original and organic to his personality, it was impossible not to be charmed by them. He made little things, like whittled wooden animals and seashell creatures. He also made big things. He'd clear a spot in the middle of dense forest to plant a garden and build a homestead, even cut down and milled trees to frame up his own tavern once. Big or small, each of Loyd's creations shared his 1970s timber man aesthetic. His self-made life was steeped in an odd combination of rustic logger practicality, honky-tonk hardship, dirty hippie mysticism, beach town kitsch, and carney mobility. Somehow it all worked. People were always enchanted by Loyd's creations.

Loyd wasn't much to brag about. My dad wasn't a war hero. Maybe he should've been— he was a natural fighter and often invited the pain and glory of conflict. But his mom was a Jehovah's Witness and Witnesses don't serve in the military. Loyd wasn't a proud athlete or great scientist. He did nothing to influence the course of history or even the politics of the rural towns he lived in. Loyd didn't work a nine-to-five job. He didn't pay bills or child support. He didn't have a phone or mailing address. My dad never met my teachers or interviewed boys before they could date me. He didn't drive me to school or teach me to drive. But he did teach me to ride a bike.

I'm not sure I would define what Loyd did as *teaching*. What he did was dictate one day that I would not go inside to my mom, I would not eat, or drink, or pee, until I rode *that damn bike*. He didn't offer many instructions. Like most lessons, Loyd taught with his body.

He stood in the road, holding a bike we'd borrowed from another family in his logging outfit. I stood beside him, looking up to his eyes. The world smelled like warm pine and dry dirt. I wore pink terry cloth shorts and a tank top striped in pastels. The neat pigtails Mom had put in that morning were now a wild mess around my dusted face.

Get on the bike, Loyd said.

Determined not to disappoint my dad, I threw a leg over the bike and slid my bony ass up onto the seat. Loyd bent behind me, his chest inches from my back, his arms around my own, and his feet firm on the ground to the left side of the bike. He gripped the handlebars on the metal part, above my hands, and started running. My heart thumped its way up my throat. At full speed Loyd released the bike and yelled.

Pedal!

My feet got tangled, or couldn't find the pedals, or I froze. Every time. I fell sideways, scraped away another part of myself. Loyd jogged over, picked up the bike, and leaned it toward me.

Get on the bike.

This process repeated as the day expanded out, its boundary somehow stopping the forward motion of time. I asked for a Band-Aid for my knee because it never had the chance to stop bleeding before hitting the ground again. Loyd said no.

You can have a Band-Aid when you ride the goddamn bike.

Get on the bike changed to *Get on the goddamn bike! Pedal!* changed to *Pedal, goddammit!*

My cheeks burned and not just because of the July sun. I felt like the whole trailer park was watching, other kids peeking out from behind the trunks of Doug firs to witness my humiliating failure. Pure metallic hate for my dad slid around my heart. I was sure it would become solid and forever.

The road was paved but breaking up and rutted, covered in scree. After each fall, I stole a few moments to pluck gravel from my skin and try to look pathetic before Loyd urged me back onto the bike. My palms and knees stung from smacking down on the road. What began as physical pain traveled inside my body and turned to burning thoughts. I wanted Loyd to be wounded as I was, wished for the strength to make him feel stung. But that was before I actually pedaled.

When I landed my feet on both pedals and felt myself pushing that bike forward, the cloud of anger and shame cleared away. I was riding that goddamned bike. My exhaustion evaporated and pedaling came as natural to me as running. The bike was an extension of my body. I understood why Loyd smiled like an idiot when he leaned his own bike into a slow, wide turn and called out for my big brother, Jesse, to follow. Until this moment, I'd always stood at the edge of our patch of grass and watched them ride together. But now Loyd was standing and watching me, now I was riding. Loyd whooped his joy.

Well, I'll be damned! he yelled. That's it, honey, you got it! Sure. As. Shit.

This time, I didn't mind that the whole neighborhood might hear.

It was like there was this whole other Tina I didn't even know existed. This Tina could power a mighty machine and get places, fast. She could escape bad guys or rob a gas station or win a race, who knows? All I knew for sure was that I was gonna ride that bike until dark and maybe even after. Never mind the trickle of blood down my shin or the raging thirst that, moments ago, I thought would kill me. Now I thrust through the warm evergreen air, I created the breeze that dried my sweat and made my scalp tingle, and I liked it. Love for my daddy swelled my chest, which made me even lighter, faster. Love for the salty tears on my face, love for the sting of my scrapes. I knew Loyd had given me a new sort of magic. Power. Then he barked at me again.

Sweetheart, get inside and get cleaned up. You look like hell.

((((

After our family broke apart, Loyd often disappeared. All my life he had on-again, off-again relationships with Alcoholics Anonymous, the Kingdom Hall, and his children. When we did see him, it was familiar and easy. We shifted into our roles. It was like riding a bike. Our bodies remembered so we didn't need to think about it. Sure, there was an initial awkwardness when Loyd came back to us. But it never took long to remember how to be with my dad.

Loyd would plan ahead for our time together. He always started off with good intentions. One summer, when I was maybe eight or nine, he had some bikes waiting for us. He'd borrowed them from a buddy whose kids had outgrown them. We got to keep them the entire time we stayed with Loyd. He wanted to ride bikes all summer because he'd bought himself a bicycle and it was his new love.

It wasn't new, but it was new to Loyd. He was ridiculously proud of this bike. It was old but Loyd had fixed it up and polished it to a shine. Looking back, I can see how the bike, like his garden, had something to do with the way his body seemed to need work. My dad always had to be striving in some way. When he lived in less traditional shelters, as he often did, the daily business of living, basic survival, was physical work. He always needed to repair, reinforce, and patch up the rustic shelters he built.

This particular summer, the summer with Loyd's beloved bike, he was renting a tidy little farmhouse in a sparsely populated neighborhood on the edge of Yakima. The house rarely needed his attention, but he had a huge garden to tend and he was always fiddling with that bike.

The bike had wide handlebars, gleaming in the sun, with red and white plastic tassels at the ends, and a cream-colored banana seat. It came with an old-fashioned, silver bicycle bell and Loyd had added his own noisemaker, one of those horns with a red bulb on the end that makes a honk like a clown's nose. This was the BMX era, so Jesse and I thought the whole thing was silly and outdated. It looked like a giant child's bike, so it fit Loyd for sure. He was childlike, irrepressible and bursting with energy in moments of joy or anger.

The thing with Loyd is you could always see everything in his face. He didn't hide his feelings, good or bad. And when he rode that bike up and down the street, he just beamed out at the world. He'd cruise along, honking his horn, ringing his bell, and hollering at us because everything seemed funny and needed to be shared. If my stepmom, Linda, came outside while he was riding by, he might yell, *Hubba Hubba!* or mimic Hank Williams as he sang out the chorus to "Hey Good Lookin." If he happened to ride near us at the right moment, he'd lift up one butt cheek to an exaggerated height and let loose a fart in our direction. Half the time I didn't even feel like riding bikes, but I always went along anyway just to be with Loyd and see how his face would light up. I was taking something away from that bike ride that had nothing to do with riding bikes.

(((((

I have a scar on my shin that I've always clung to as evidence of my first bike-riding lesson with Loyd. Truth is that scar could've come from some other fall. That memory, like so many, is unreliable. I can't say for sure what town we lived in when he taught me to ride a bike. Just like I can't be sure we were in Yakima the summer he had his vintage bike with the clown horn. Jesse can't say either, though he thinks I learned to ride a bike in Randle. Mom isn't sure if I learned before she left Loyd or after. It's difficult to place memories in a childhood of migrations.

This is what it was like to be Loyd's daughter. I was always collecting evidence, memorizing moments, eavesdropping on stories, trying to hold on to what happened, when, and how. Proof that I had a dad and that he was fun and silly and I was important to him. Sometimes, my imagination filled in the blank spots.

When I stand in the first bike memory, I feel the aura of Loyd's place in Yakima. But that doesn't fit because I was too old that summer. I already knew how to ride a bike by then. Maybe he taught me in Clallam Bay? Morton? Seiku? Loyd was a drifter. We rarely lived in the same place twice.

When I was with my dad, my stories always had different settings, so my mind sometimes puts me on that bike in different towns, Loyd running beside me on different streets.

The truth of this story, like so many things about my dad, is lost to me. Maybe that's why I need to set him down on paper, keep him from disappearing altogether. Because sometimes, it feels like he never existed at all, like I made him up entirely.

But I didn't make Loyd. He made me. That day on the bike is just one of many ways he made me. I suppose this was Loyd's legacy. He left nothing much physical behind on this earth. No poetry or paintings, no endowments or discoveries to share with humankind. There are some photos, letters he wrote to us kids. Mostly his existence was primal flashes of intensity in different places, always a sense of adventure and danger. There was a sort of balance to his living, creativity and destruction in equal measure. Always harm. Always love.

For many years, I'd think of the bike-riding lesson and only see my bloody knee, only feel the purple indents left on the palms of my hands by gravel. I'd taste sweat and tears and snot and the acid of my anger. Now I wonder, how did I manage to forget the power I felt when I first rode that bike? Nothing in this story was mine—not the bike, the neighborhood, the friends, the house. Sometimes, most of the time, not even the dad. They'd all be lost to poverty, addiction, and Loyd's migrations. But I had this new ability and it belonged to me. It was only mine. I could ride a bike. Why did I let myself forget the freedom and the flying?

timber child

WHEN I WAS BORN, my mom brought me home from the hospital in a cardboard box. After she told me that, I thought it made a lot of sense. Like it says something about what sort of life this kid should expect. But it turns out cardboard baby containers were pretty common in hospitals in 1976. They came flat and perforated, to be folded into a sort of temporary baby bed. Mom's nurse at Clearwater Valley Hospital swaddled me up, tucked me into that box, and sent us on our way. Mom was hurting from the surgery but anxious to get home to Jesse before Loyd started celebrating the Fourth of July and things got rowdy. She set me on the bench seat next to her and began her hour-long drive to Headquarters. My little box slid out of her reach at the first corner, and I came to rest against the passenger door.

Mom was right to be worried. By the time she got home, Loyd had managed to blow up a string of firecrackers stowed away in Jesse's pocket. Lucky my brother had taken his hoodie off and left it lying in the dirt because, by the time Loyd realized he'd lit the wrong fuse, that sweatshirt was toast. For Loyd, Independence Day was for lighting *firepoppers,* day drinking with his buddies, and howling at the moon. He didn't see a new baby or recovering wife as reasons to settle down. If anything, he had more to celebrate.

I can smell that smoky day, like many more to come. Hot dogs roasting over campfire, cigarettes, the sulfur tang of fireworks. I can see Jesse with his face dug into a wide slice of watermelon, like a green and red smile stretching beyond his chin. Loyd would let him salt it himself and encourage him to spit watermelon seeds into the fire *like a man*. I can hear Loyd burn his finger by holding on to a bottle rocket too long. *Sonofabitch! That thing's hotter than a popcorn fart!* He'd always light fireworks then stand right there, waiting until the last possible minute to run to safety.

Mom says it didn't take long for me to compete with Loyd's whooping and hollering. He lit off a string of firecrackers and the sharp *crack! crack! crack!* started me wailing. I didn't stop much for a few months. Mom was never sure if that was colic, or just that I got scared so bad right out of the gate like that. She nearly wore a hole in the floor of our fifteen-foot camper trailer, pacing the length of it for three months, trying to soothe my crying.

We were a timber family so, for me, it all started in the woods. Columbia Helicopters was lifting trees out of north Idaho and Loyd was hired on as a loader operator. Working in helicopter logging had a sort of status. You had to be skilled to make it on a Columbia crew and Loyd was proud of that. He followed work across that land of elk, wolves, and salmon, cutting and loading trees by day, partying with his buddies at night, and pulling his wife and kids along behind him in a camper.

Mom knew timber, too. She was born in Rescue, California, which feels like prophecy since she's rescued me countless times. By the time she met Loyd, her dad had been running a small logging outfit out of Jackson for a few years. Grandpa, known as "Pothead" because he wore a wide cowboy hat said to look like a toilet, would've liked a bunch of sons to work the outfit. But it took him and Grandma Thelma nine girls before they managed to produce one boy. They had so many girls they gave a couple away. When another girl followed their only son, they quit trying. Pothead made do with his daughters on the crew. Mom spent her seventeenth summer *driving logging truck* alongside her sister, Ruth, who got to drive the Cat because she was older. Just a couple years later, Mom met Loyd at a barbecue full of loggers.

His eyes and his smile worked on her. He had green eyes, as if the forest had marked him. Loyd's eyes lit so bright when he smiled, you'd think somebody had flipped a switch. That smile was a trick since Loyd had no natural teeth by the time he met Mom. His genes predisposed him to cavities, substance abuse, and fighting. All are hard on the teeth. Loyd kept losing teeth until finally, at age nineteen, he decided they weren't worth all the headache. One payday, he walked into a dentist's office with a pocketful of cash. He told that dentist to yank what was left and set him up with *a new set of chompers* that couldn't rot out.

Loyd's false teeth were straight, white, and plopped into a jar each night for cleaning. Jesse and I loved to play with our dad's cheeks when he took his teeth out, leaving his face slack and pliable. From earliest days, I remember reaching up to push my dad's face around like it was Play-Doh. I can see his smile and hear his muffled chuckle, the exhale pushing through his nose. He was granting us that particular brand of gentle tolerance we all reserve for the very young.

Loyd's bright eyes and crooked smile charmed Mom so hard that she missed the warning signs. Just a few months later she was married and pregnant but living without a husband while Loyd served out a six-month jail sentence for stealing a chainsaw. He'd been leaving the tavern late one night and right there in the parking lot was a shiny new Stihl sitting in the back of a pickup truck. Maybe sober he would've walked on by, but his old friend Jack Daniels made the solid point that only a fool leaves a brand-new chainsaw sitting out like that around a bunch of drunks and woodcutters. Loyd nabbed it and walked away like nothing. Soon, he was going around town using the stolen saw in plain sight, finally using it one day to buck up a tree that had fallen in an old lady's yard. The woman couldn't pay but Loyd *wasn't about to leave no ol' lady in a bind, no way, no how.* Too bad that old lady was neighbors with the saw's rightful owner. He saw Loyd using his Stihl, fresh orange chain cover sitting in the dirt, and called the police. Cops showed up before Loyd was even done bucking that tree.

((((

I was born on the move, just like my dad. We were lumber nomads, native to nowhere. Loyd was born in Klamath Falls, where Grandpa Herb worked at a sawmill for a while. When it came time for me to join my family, we were set up in Headquarters, but it just as easily could have been another timber town. Headquarters isn't even officially a town. It's unincorporated, a company town at the end of the Camas Prairie Railroad. But it used to bustle with timber families, used by logging outfits as a place to set up camp while they harvested in the area. Today the Pacific Northwest logging industry is a ghost of what it once was and the same can be said for Headquarters.

I imagine our trailer in Headquarters, the hitch sitting up on blocks, in a circle of dry reddish dirt. I can see other trailers nearby and towering over them all, a forest of Douglas fir, western hemlock, and western red cedar. Standing in this clearing, this grove of trailers, I smell those evergreens warming in the sun as they watch over the flow of migrating families. I smell extinguished campfires and hear the faraway whine of chainsaws, the constant chatter of birds, and insects clicking their songs. If it's daytime I hear the rhythmic work of a woodpecker searching for food. At night, I hear frogs, crickets, and faint evidence of running water. I might see a few permanent structures in the camp, a laundry or an office, maybe.

Sloan, a lean German shepherd mix, is tied to the front hitch of our trailer. He has created a patch of worn earth, packed down by his paws as he runs back and forth on his lead. That dog will inspire my first sentence. *Shut up, Sloan!* A fact that so tickles Loyd, he'll often entice the dog to bark just to hear my toddler voice repeat it. Loyd made Sloan's lead from a repurposed length of yellow nylon winch strap. Loyd always talked about Sloan like he was best dog a man could want. Said he was gentle with us kids, but also a fierce and protective scrapper. He'd fight for us if he needed to. Mom remembered Sloan different. To her, he was another life to care for, another expense we couldn't afford, a constant source of guilt. Always chained up, cowering under the trailer in thunderstorms or when fireworks or guns went off.

A couple of lawn chairs, with frames of metal tubing, sit outside the door of the trailer. Their seats sunk from constant use, their backs woven of wide plastic bands in white and green. They have avocado platform arm-rests and surround the firepit. This is my first home, the first of many.

Wood paneling covers the inside walls and cabinets. A child can see the world in wood paneling. She can find shapes in the fabricated knots and lines to represent all the things she might never actually see. The kitchen has orange countertops with aluminum edges. Yellow linoleum, with an orange and brown pattern to simulate tile, meets the small patches of dark brown carpet in the sleeping and living areas at either end. The table, push-ing up out of the floor like a square mushroom, folds flat to make the bed my brother and I share at night. At first, Mom puts me in a car bed and Jesse lies next to it until I'm old enough to snuggle in beside him.

During the day, our bed becomes the table again and holds a heavy glass ashtray filled with cigarette butts. As a toddler, I sometimes climb on the bench seat and lean across the table to smell the ashtray. The table edge digs between my tiny ribs. My elbows crunch as I force my weight on them, straining toward what has been placed out of my reach. I extend my legs and stretch to put my nose at the lip of the amber-colored glass and gently sniff, the smell a concentrated comfort until I am old enough to be ashamed of it. Yellow cotton blankets are folded to line both bench seats. I like to run their satin edging between my thumb and forefinger, to pick off the little fiber pills that spatter their surfaces. On the counter is my mom's coffee cup, brownish-gold ceramic but somehow metallic. A pattern of raised bumps, like an army of uniform warts, marches around its center. I like to run the pads of my fingers over them and pretend they're telling me something in code. Later, after we left Loyd and I started school far away from him, I would think of my dad and this set of coffee cups when I learned about Helen Keller and the magic way she learned to read stories with her fingertips.

(((((((((

Headquarters was so small that Mom had to go to a doctor in Orofino, about an hour's drive away. She'd had trouble giving birth to Jesse two and a half years before, so there was no question all her babies would come into this world via C-section. At a checkup late in her pregnancy, the doctor found that Mom and I are Rh incompatible. He didn't expect Rh factor would cause any harm to my mom or me. But it would trigger her body's immune response against Rh and make future pregnancies dangerous. Mom needed two shots, one before I was delivered and one immediately after. Sounds simple enough, but each shot was made from donated blood.

Mom signed the consent form for treatment, but Loyd wouldn't. His mom, Billie, had been a devout Jehovah's Witness. She died at age forty-two, just two years after giving birth herself. Loyd had a tenuous attachment to his mother's religion, but he sometimes imposed the doctrine on us. When I was born, the Watchtower Society discouraged its flock from accepting blood products for medical treatment. Loyd's ability to walk the righteous path ebbed and flowed. Kingdom Hall meetings usually correlated with his AA attendance. Loyd wasn't sober when I was born. Still, when Mom went in for surgery, he decided it was the Lord's will that she should not receive a blood product. In 1976, Clearwater Valley Hospital wouldn't give her the treatment she requested without her husband's consent.

Mom decided she wanted her tubes tied. If she couldn't protect future babies from harm, she'd prevent future babies altogether. Again Clearwater Valley required Loyd's signature and again he denied it. He said it would be too easy for Mom to screw around on him if she didn't have to worry about getting knocked up. Always seemed like Loyd's big fear was his wife cheating. Funny, since he's the one who had trouble keeping it in his pants. Loyd kept expecting the worst of himself from other people. To show Mom and the doctor that he was reasonable, he had a vasectomy.

(((

Grandma Billie died before I was born. Still, she was like a mythical character in my bedtime stories. The way Loyd told it, she was a perfect wife and mother who stood guard over me with the power of an angel and the ferocity of a grandmother. In my mind, the image of my dead grandma watching over me got all mixed up with the pictures on the covers of the *Watchtower* pamphlets scattered through my childhood. Green pastures, blue skies with a pure white cloud or two, smiling people, and grazing sheep all existed in tepid harmony on those booklets. I came to think there was an actual watchtower in that place. It followed that Grandma Billie was in that tower and could see me from her highest window. Like a princess locked away, awaiting rescue.

Grandma Billie's religion was a handy excuse Loyd used to control his wife and kids. But I think that need for control was mostly the work of his own father. Grandpa Herb is a kind memory to me. He had a soft voice and what I thought was a sweet southern drawl. He was handsome, with a head of dark, thick hair that never seemed to gray. I only ever saw him dressed in button-up shirts, flannel in winter and cotton in summer, under denim overalls. He wore a wide-brimmed cowboy hat and cheap tennis shoes. I never heard him raise his voice or saw him raise his hand.

Turns out Grandpa wasn't so gentle in younger days, particularly toward his family. He had some pretty firm thoughts about keeping his house in order, his wife and kids in line. He also felt strongly about owner-ship, property, and legal rights for women. Herb taught his sons you *don't never put a woman's name on a title, deed, or account of any kind*. Grandma Billie didn't own her house or car. She had to ask for her husband's signa-ture to write a check, get cash from the bank, even buy groceries.

When I came into this world, our nation was celebrating its bicenten-nial. Loyd bought a commemorative silver dollar, drilled a hole in it, and wore it on a leather cord around his neck so he could always carry a piece of me. That same year, wolves were listed as endangered in Idaho so biol-ogists started a plan to catch and release mating pairs from Canada. Snake River wildlife managers also got concerned about the low numbers of fish returning to spawn. They decided to limit salmon and steelhead fishing to try and recover what Pacific Northwest dams and overfishing had cost us all. Man pushed fish and wolves toward extinction, creating an oppor-tunity to save them. Mom wasn't allowed medical treatment without her husband's permission. It all feels connected—the wolves, the salmon, my mom. All were being managed in Idaho in 1976. I wonder about how we decide what, or who, is property. How we manage what belongs to us.

(((

Mom always wanted a little girl and planned to call her Rebecca Lynne. Jesse had been a happy surprise but she planned me and I always found that idea kind of precious. My mom imagined me first, then made me. I was intentional. Most kids I knew were made first and sometimes never imagined at all.

When I came along, Loyd decided he didn't like the name Rebecca. If Loyd told the story of my naming, he'd say he felt it was his turn to name a kid, since Mom had picked Jesse's name. He'd let that statement sit in such a way that I understood it had mysterious weight. Wasn't until I was fully grown that I learned that Jesse was already a baby when Mom met Loyd. She'd graduated high school with Jesse in her tummy and Loyd could never quite forgive her for letting some other man father his son. Loyd's little jabs at Mom were the only hints I ever got about it. Anyone could see that Jesse was Loyd's son and that Loyd loved his boy *somethin' fierce.*

Tina Marie was the name of a little girl in our trailer park and she was always making Loyd laugh with her shenanigans. He figured the name would work just fine for his own baby girl. So I was born in a place I don't remember and named after someone who is a stranger to me.

Just before it was time to move to a new job site, Loyd crashed our '55 Chevy Nomad. He'd gone to town to shoot pool and drove into a creek on the way home. He had to have it pulled out and fixed in a hurry so we'd be ready to pull the trailer and follow the outfit. We really couldn't afford the expense, but Mom was so ready to get out of Headquarters she didn't argue.

(((

When I was four months old, we were living in Hoopa, California, and Mom got worried about a wheezing in my chest. She outlawed smoking in the trailer, but I didn't get better. Turns out I'd developed pneumonia. I had to be hospitalized and that was hard on her. The hospital couldn't make exceptions to visiting hours, even for the mother of a small baby, so she had to leave me there alone each night.

Hoopa was another unincorporated town, this one on the reservation of the Hupa people. As Loyd told it, his outfit was logging on Hupa land and the tribe wasn't happy about it. Mom doesn't remember it that way. But Loyd claimed that each morning he had to pass through a peaceful protest line of tribal members trying to keep loggers off their ancestral lands. He said he felt real bad about it, *but a man's gotta feed his family.* Loyd got the idea in his head that maybe I got sick because of a curse on the loggers.

Loyd perpetuated all sorts of everyday myths, like the idea that a daddy longlegs spider was deadly poisonous but its mouth too small to bite people, or that you get warts from touching frogs. I was terrified of swallowing watermelon seeds because he seemed sure that a watermelon plant would grow in my belly, a vine reaching up and out my mouth, if I did. Loyd loved the possibility of ancient Indian magic. He teased Mom's anxiety with his theory because my nurses were mostly members of the Hupa tribe. Even as a young kid I was uneasy with the way Loyd told this story. The way Mom's energy shifted every time made me know there was something wrong with his telling. Something so deep we couldn't talk plain about it because we didn't have the words.

According to Loyd, Mom left me every evening in tears and tossed through the night, worried the nurses might take revenge against the logging outfit by letting her baby girl die. Loyd would tell this story like it was the Wild West or something. Mom always seemed ashamed of his version. When she heard Loyd tell it to me like that, she'd make sure to add a quiet aside, letting me know those nurses gave me excellent care, even took turns holding me on their breaks, and left colorful toys and gifts around my crib. She told me I healed faster because of their kindness.

Not long after I was released from the hospital, we left Loyd. I think it was the first time but can't be sure. Problem is, Loyd would get to drinking and drugging and that led to hitting. Mom was sort of used to that—her own daddy was a hitter. But sometimes, enough is enough. After a particularly hard night, she figured it was time. She loaded up Jesse and me while Loyd was at work and drove the five or so hours to her mom.

Loyd came home that day, realized we were gone, and got worked up. Letting his wife walk out on him was not the sort of thing he was raised to do. He started hauling our stuff outside. Toys, clothes, pictures, even my baby book. Anything Mom left behind that could cause her hurt. He lit it all on fire and watched it burn. For years, they'd tell me my baby pictures burned up in a storage fire. In fact, Loyd set himself to destroying what he thought he couldn't have.

Once he sobered up, he came begging for Mom to come home. Promised he'd get sober and even try to satisfy her want for staying in one place. This was an expectation that hung heavy over our household, that Loyd would find stable work, another company job or millwork maybe, so we could settle in one place before Jesse started school. He promised he'd make it happen, so we went back. Mom bought an empty baby book for me and tried to fill it in from memory but it's still pretty sparse.

We were back in Clearwater County for my first birthday so I pretty much spent my first year migrating, back to where I started. Mom said I had the flu pretty bad the day I turned one, but she still invited some of the camp kids over and they brought gifts. I'm not sure how she got away with a birthday celebration, since we didn't celebrate Christmas the first few years of my life so I'm pretty sure Loyd was sticking with the Jehovah's Witness stuff back then. Sometimes, Loyd's attempts to get right with the Lord felt deeply sincere, other times they just felt convenient. Like when we were too broke for Christmas and birthday gifts, or when Loyd could use doctrine to control Mom. All I know is there were long periods when the Kingdom Hall wasn't part of our lives at all.

We lived in a one-room studio in Sandpoint, Idaho, for a few months. Not long after we settled into the place, Loyd forgot his promise to Mom and went out and got drunk with his buddies. Mom got tired waiting up for him so she locked the door and went to bed. She was curled up asleep with Jesse and me when Loyd came home and found the door locked. Already in a violent mood, he took that locked door as an insult. Mom woke to him yelling and beating on the door and windows. He asked if she had another man in there. Standing at the door, she told him through the glass he could come home when he'd sobered up. Now that really pissed him off. A man works all day to pay the rent and here she is telling him when he can come and go. He punched right through the window and reached inside, trying to unlock the doorknob. Mom grabbed her cast iron skillet off the stove and smacked his hand before she even had time to think. Once she'd done that, she knew she better keep him out. That studio was just too small to hold his anger without us kids getting hurt. Every time he'd reach back in, she'd hit him again. His hands were bloody when the cops came and hauled him off. He had to get stitches, but Mom's not sure if that's from the skillet or from Loyd punching through the glass.

I don't remember being a baby. I have no flashes of my mother gazing down into my cradle or my father lifting me up over his head to let me feel the power of flight before I could even walk, though I'm sure those things did happen. It's difficult to report on imperfect memory, but what I do know from those years comes from a different sort of memory. We all have intrinsic memory, a fusion of the stories we've heard and physical immersion in our family atmosphere. Our early environment documents the past in our bodies like rings in an old-growth cedar. A salmon knows her river of birth by some mysterious recall, soaked into her during the very formation of her body. That's the way I know our years of migration, through osmosis.

I know my mother, beautiful and quiet. Her tobacco hair, long and parted in the middle, her face an olive. I know the small silver watch around her thin wrist as she lifted a coffee cup to her lips, pointer finger through the handle. She held her cigarette like a princess holds up the skirt of her gown. I can hear the timbre of her voice, the calm tone she'd use to talk Loyd down from an angry height, keep him from jumping down and landing on us all. I know her innate sense of propriety, a force that eventually pushed her toward another life. She's a storyteller but in those years, she kept her stories close. There was only room for one maker in our small trailer and that was Loyd. He cracked jokes and we laughed. He whittled toys and we played with them. He needed to create. Mom bided her time as healer, caregiver. She held us when the only thing he could make was fear. Or worse.

I know my daddy, sun chapped and hard. Not a big man, but a very strong one. All wiry muscle and energy. His nose crooked ever since he'd had it broken on a pool table in Wenatchee. Loyd's voice was a little high-pitched and he had the faintest trace of a drawl, connecting him back to Alabama and Louisiana. Early mornings, he liked to sit quiet and think. I can see him sitting on the bench seat at our fold-out table, drinking his Folgers with three heaping spoonfuls of sugar from a milky green ceramic cup. His cheek is near the foggy window, droplets of rain on the outside, and he's looking out while the lazy smoke from his cigarette floats up from the big amber ashtray to circle his face.

When he was feeling less peaceful, Loyd didn't like to be bored. He was always taking Jesse and me on walks, teaching us card games, whittling with us. On a rainy day he might gather up a coffee cup and a clothespin and we'd take turns carrying the clothespin across the length of the trailer between our knees to drop it in the coffee cup on the other end. He'd cobble up a prize of some sort if we won, a piece of candy or a nickel maybe. He liked to make physical contact. He never walked by without reaching to touch us on the head or shoulder. He had specific ways he'd connect with each of us, too. He'd play football or baseball with Jesse and take him out to help work on the car or stack wood. Before I was even off the bottle Loyd figured out that I shared his taste for salty foods. He'd pull out a can of kippered snacks and call me over to crawl into his lap and share. We'd eat dill pickles straight from the jar while Loyd cracked jokes about his high school girlfriend, Mona Pickle. I learned from Loyd how to make popcorn in a soup pot on the stovetop. When the popping slowed, he'd tip the lid in quick bursts and throw in pats of butter while the steam pushed out at our faces. Then he'd carefully transfer the pot to my grip and tell me to dance. I'd jump around and shake it in front of my body then Loyd would take it away and dump it out into a huge silver bowl and wave the saltshaker over it. He'd make a big deal of testing it, to see if I did a good job getting the popcorn tossed in all that butter. I still make it like that.

(((

Loyd never read books to us. I think he was ashamed of his poor literacy. But he liked telling us stories and in Loyd's hands, all stories were funny. Many of my own memories are mixed up with the version Loyd told. Most he'd tell as comedy, even though I remembered them as sad or scary. I was often confused by Loyd's interpretation.

He had a handful of adventures he'd go back to again and again. Most were logging stories. Like the time he nearly killed himself because he ignored a basic rule everyone knows—never stand downhill when you crosscut. Loyd and his brother, our Uncle Papa, would cut thick slabs from giant tree trunks left behind by logging operations. They'd lacquer these big crosscut slabs, put legs on them, and sell them as coffee tables. Often, they'd pull out big knots to create deep crevices and drop in pocket change, dice, maybe even a Matchbox car, before sealing the whole thing up. They'd go forage at logging sites to find stumps. Loyd was out alone one day, working his way through a tree trunk as wide as a Volkswagen. *This sucker was so huge I found myself in need of some serious leverage. I knew damn well I was putting my leg in the wrong place, but goddamn I was so close and just ready to get outta them woods for the day, I tell you what.*

So Loyd was low, right knee under him on the ground, left leg extended downhill, boot heel dug into the earth to keep him stable while he put his whole weight into the blade. He broke through sooner than expected and knew in a split second he was in trouble. He pulled back quick as a nervous rabbit but not before the buzzing teeth of his saw sank into his inner thigh. *Now, kids, you might think that was a bloody mess but it wasn't that bad at first. I mean it was bleeding, no doubt, but didn't seem like nothin' I couldn't handle on my own. Hardly hurt at all. Still, I had the sense to call it quits, figured I'd be back to haul that slab out later.* Loyd decided to go think about the best course of action over a cup of coffee.

Loyd's sister, our Aunt Rainy, was working at the café in Packwood in those days. He limped in, sat down, and Aunt Rainy walked over with the coffeepot. But when she saw the blood soaking through his pants she *about had a shit fit, right there.* Aunt Rainy utilized her right to refuse service.

Bro, she said, I'll bring you pancakes and bacon once you've seen the doctor, but I ain't giving you even a drop of coffee 'til you get that leg checked out.

Kids, your Aunt Rainy mighta saved my skinny ass that day, and I ain't pullin' your leg. I'll be damned if that doctor didn't tell me I coulda died from that cut. Turns out there's a pretty big blood pipe runs through my damn leg, right here. I had more stitches than Frankenstein, but I was fine so I went back for my coffee and hotcakes. Still had blood all over my pants but I sat there, grinning at your Aunt Rainy, and ate them like it was nothin'. Afterward, he went back to get his wood slab.

My favorite was the story about the day Loyd popped his eye out in the woods. He was packing out his saw at the end the day when it happened. He was last man out, thinking about catching up to his buddies to grab a beer before heading home, as he picked his path through the thick litter of the forest floor.

I can see this scene—that was the trick of Loyd's stories. He always set them up with a simple hook, something true and clear I automatically trusted. He knew his audience. We were timber children so this story had a beginning so familiar we could picture it right off. We knew Loyd packed his saw out on his left shoulder, always. We knew the blade would lay flat and steady over the space between his neck and his shoulder, and run out in front of him as if leading the way. The motor just behind him, cased in hard orange plastic, his left hand flung up over the blade, the crook of his elbow against the chain, keeping the saw steady for his hike out. I knew the way my dad packed his saw out of the woods like I knew the sound of my own breath from inside my head. I could even smell Loyd—sweat, sawdust, gasoline—and hear the snapping of his feet breaking a thousand unknown things with each step. This image was truth.

Loyd said he was packing out his saw when he put his black, steel-toed boot down and it sank into forest flotsam and landed, with full weight of man and saw, on a branch fallen from above. *It was a big one—if I'd a been standing there when it fell, it coulda been a widow-maker.* The branch was too strong to snap so when Loyd stepped on it, he created a fulcrum and seesawed it up to his own face like a bad cartoon. A farmer stepping on a rake as he chases a naughty rabbit caught eating his carrot patch.

That branch couldn't have been a better length to do him damage. He said it came right up and gouged his eye clean out. *I shit you not, that sucker just poked right in there at the corner of my eye and, pop! Before I knew it, my goddamned eye was hanging out in fronta my face and I was in a worlda hurt.*

I had so many questions here, questions I never asked because from earliest days I understood my role in maintaining Loyd's fictions. *Daddy misses you, Daddy's sorry, Daddy wishes your momma would let him see you, Daddy's gonna come get you just as soon as he gets a car, a paycheck, a break from work.* Still, I wanted to know so many things. I wondered if his eye could see anything, as it lay there, suspended by tendrils never meant to know open air. I wondered if that eye sent images to his brain, of the leafy bracken below, or maybe his own cheek, lips, chin. I always at least half believed Loyd and if there was any chance this story was true, I wanted to know what that eye saw from its foreign angle. But I never asked. Too many details might expose the story as fiction and I didn't want to let go of the possibility of truth.

Loyd stood there gauging his options. He was alone in the forest, chainsaw on his left shoulder, metal lunch pail in his right hand, thermos tucked into his right armpit, right eye dangling on top of his cheekbone, and a couple of miles to go before he was literally out of the woods. *Kids, a man's gotta do what a man's gotta do.*

He squatted down, dropped his lunch pail and thermos, set his Stihl on the ground, and went about the awkward business of handling his loose eye with dirty, calloused hands. My dad had hands with their own incredible landscapes. There were soft sandy beaches and dry, scorched deserts on those hands. There were cracks so deep that black grease had seeped in to create permanent lines, marking out the boundaries between all the territories of his hands. And here he was, about to cup his exposed eyeball in a greasy, sweaty palm, about to use his rough fingers, coated in sawdust painted on with oil, gasoline, pre-mix, to gingerly touch his vulnerable, precious eyeball.

Well, kids, right then I figured, aw hell, can a man fall trees with only one eye? I wasn't sure. I just knew I couldn't fall trees if I died before getting outta them woods, so I had to do something and I'll be damned if I'm gonna leave my saw behind. So I put this part of my palm up under that eye and just shoved it back in. It hurt like a sonofabitch but what else could I do?

Loyd didn't try to open the eye. He didn't even want to think what that might feel like and he'd had enough trauma in the woods for one day. He hefted his saw back up on his shoulder, tucked his thermos back into his armpit, grabbed his lunch pail, and finished packing himself out with that eye shut the whole time. *Man alive, my pickup sure was a sight for sore eye.* He threw his saw in the bed, set everything else on the bench seat, jumped in, and headed straight for the hospital. It was the only time in his life he took himself to a doctor without some woman hollering at him to do so.

According to Loyd, the doctor could see no course of action but to pop the eye back out. They needed to clean out the sawdust and whatnot Loyd had gotten up in there. He had to hang his head over a stainless-steel basin so his eye could float in some saline mixture until the doctor was satisfied it was clean. Then, that doctor popped Loyd's eye back into the socket, good as new.

Loyd's eyes were beautiful, and I always loved looking in my daddy's hazel-green eyes. Good or bad, his eyes told you exactly what he was thinking and where he was headed. I knew by looking at his eyes if I should run toward him or run away. Loyd's eyes are my eyes, though I always thought they were more magic on his face than mine. After he told us that story, I was always lingering on the right eye, trying to find evidence to back his story, but it looked the same as it ever had.

something to cry about

I WAS TOO YOUNG FOR MEMORY in our vagabond years. My dad created my history of that time, so I came to think of myself as pretty damn special. Because anytime Loyd told a story about Jesse or me, the moral was always the same—your daddy loves you.

Tina Marie, you damn near drowned when you was nothing more than two feet high and I swear I thought I'd just jump in that water and drown along with you, and I ain't lyin'.

Mom started to feel claustrophobic with all four of us crammed into that fifteen-foot trailer so she convinced Loyd to upgrade. They sold the camper and the Nomad and bought a thirty-five-footer and a pickup truck to haul it. Mom called the new trailer *the Mansion.*

We were moving again and had just pulled into a trailer park in Oroville, California. I guess you could say that Oroville is a place for miracles. It was a gold rush town and home to California's oldest orange tree, The Mother Orange. It's also the place where the last known Yahi man was captured in 1908, a miracle to the anthropologists who studied him. I don't imagine the captured man thought that was much a miracle. All depends on who tells the story.

Jesse and I were fussy after hours in the truck. Mom let us run around while she and Loyd talked with the manager of the trailer park about a spot for the Mansion. Loyd considered himself of particular wisdom when it came to picking a campsite. He wanted it just right. If it was up to Mom, we'd be near the laundry, bathrooms, main road, or playground. But Loyd picked a site using his own set of mysterious criteria.

Loyd walked around empty camping spots like a water witch, as if he could sense some force the rest of us couldn't. If there was a creek, he'd pick a site near it because everybody sleeps better when they can hear water falling down a mountain and that's just a fact. If there was a mountain, meadow, or other view worth having, it would win over convenience every time. Loyd might like a patch of sun, so he could grow tomatoes or cucumbers, but he'd give that up for a primo spot deep in the woods where he could make noise without pestering neighbors. *Sometimes, a man's just gotta let 'er rip, right, Jess?* He was imagining how we'd spend our time, the proximity of fire pit to door, where the light would come in to kiss our faces in the morning.

Jesse and I followed along, orbiting our parents while they moved from site to site, letting Loyd do his thing. Mom and Loyd were talking with the landlord when Mom's ears perked, her eyebrows pulled together. *Your mama knew right off something was up. She just froze like a doe when she hears a crack in the woods.*

Mom turned to check on us and saw Jesse playing alone. No Tina in sight. She knelt down in front of Jesse, put her hands on his shoulders, and gave him her serious tone.

Where is your sister? He didn't know. She stood and called my name.

What's up? Loyd asked. Mom looked at the landlord.

My daughter, she said. She's only two . . .

According to Loyd, that landlord looked real scared when he said, There's a pool! The landlord pointed and started running. *But I'll tell you what, sweetheart, Daddy left that sucker in his dust. I ran like a bat outta hell. You'd a thought a mountain lion was about to bite me in the ass.*

Mom picked Jesse up—she wasn't about to lose another kid—and started jogging around, yelling my name. Loyd went straight for the pool and that's where he found me, hovering face down between the surface and the concrete bottom, painted tropical blue. Arms open, palms down, yellow hair swimming and sparkling. Everything went quiet. Loyd never knew quiet like that, said I looked like an angel floating in a summer sky. I always got a lump in my throat right here, that's how good he was at conveying the emotion he felt in that moment. Hearing Loyd tell this story, I understood how silence hits you like a solid thing then washes over you, turns to a soft blanket slowing the progress of time and the travel of air, in a moment where you witness the way life can evaporate from a body. There's a silent, infinite second where you wonder, before time starts again and you must act, if that life will be restored.

Well honey, I'm not gonna lie. By the time I got there, I thought it was too late. I figured you were a goner. You were floating there face down, your hair all up around your head, and I wondered what I'd tell your mama, if I should turn round and stop her coming so she didn't hafta see that. Man, I was afraid right then, Tina Marie, and I ain't just a woofin' ya. But Daddy knew he just had to try.

Loyd jumped in fully dressed. He misjudged my depth the first grab and missed, but took hold the second time. He brought me to the surface, confused that I could suddenly weigh so much, flipped me over his lap, and beat my back. *I'm sorry to tell ya, honey, but you had a few bruises after that. Daddy hated seeing his handprint on your little back like that.* He turned me over and pushed the water out of my lungs. I puked up pool water all over Loyd but just before he told that part, just before the story turned funny, tears would bloom up real slow in his eyes and he'd sit a minute in the sorrow of what could have been.

(((

When I was two or three, we went to Louisiana on a Greyhound bus. It was the four of us, along with Aunt Rainy and her baby girl, Tanya. According to Mom that trip was a real shit show. By the time Grandpa Herb picked us up at the station, we'd been cramped up on that bus for three days. Loyd didn't see any sense in buying me my own seat, said he'd hold me on his lap. But I got carsick early on and he lost patience with my fussing. I ended up in Mom's arms for the entire trip while she apologized for my crying and retching. Mom stepped out into the humidity of Pitkin, covered in sweat and vomit, and thought maybe we ought to stay rather than suffer that miserable ride again.

Once she met Loyd's kin she knew better. He had a pack of cousins, all about as wild as he was. As soon as we showed up, they came around looking for a good time. He went out drinking with them and Mom thought that was alright, since he hadn't seen most since childhood. But one night turned into every night, the whole lot of them running around, howling and sniffing at anything interesting. Finally, Grandpa got a call in the dark hours of morning and headed to the police station to bail Loyd out of jail. Bar fights were normal for him, but this one must've been pretty rough. When we got back on the Greyhound, Loyd had a nasty hangover and a few broken ribs. So now Mom had to two fussy babies to manage, a carsick toddler, and Loyd, sweating out booze and popping the pills his cousins had sent along for the pain.

Loyd never could mix strong emotions with alcohol. It's like the time he lost a buddy on the job. They were just about done for the day when a young cutter got crushed by shifting logs. *Coulda been any one of us. Ain't no doubt, if I'd a been standing in that same spot, I wouldn't be sitting here talking to you right now.* The boys hauled him out to the hospital as gentle as they could, but he never really made it out of the forest that day. He left behind a wife and baby girl. Loyd and the rest of the crew took it pretty hard. A man's crew is family.

That day, after the drama wore off and sad reality sank in, the women and children gathered around the young widow, began the work of coping. They showed up at her trailer with casseroles, made coffee, smoked cigarettes, took turns holding her little girl. In some ways, it was the worst any of them could imagine. In others, it was like she'd won the lottery. Death on the job meant she could settle in one place, maybe even buy a little house with the payout. She could know a life many of these women longed for— modest security without a man.

While the women tended to what he left behind, the young logger's crewmates headed to the local tavern. The boys sat around, talking shit about the dead man, cementing the images they'd carry for the rest of their lives, and drinking themselves silly. They laughed about a joke Loyd played on all the new guys. He'd ask them to grab the huge grappling hook that hung down from the chopper and hand it over to him. The metal hook carried a charge and needed to be grounded. *We would just shock the hell out of every newbie, I shit you not.* When the dead man had been initiated, he didn't whine or get bent out of shape. He took it like a real man and bought everyone a beer after work.

The night he died, the crew drank and talked but eventually grew restless. Storytelling wasn't enough to purge their grief and even worse, their guilt. Because every man who walked out of the woods felt guilty. Before long, the whole gang poured out of the bar at once. They didn't make a plan—they moved like they were called by nature, the same force that pulls salmon to the sea and wolves to prey.

In the parking lot, they pulled their chainsaws out of their rigs and piled, every one of them, into one truck. They were stuffed in the cab and the bed. Some stood leaning over the roof. Drunk and grimy from work, a few still had the dead man's blood on their sleeves, pants. They moved with the silent determination of holy men on a pilgrimage.

My mom always said there was no worse combination than Loyd, guilt, and alcohol. She learned this the hard way, with her body. It seems this was true of the whole crew that night, or maybe it was all Loyd's idea. I wouldn't be surprised. As the story goes, they got quite destructive. The next morning, the whole county woke to some serious communication difficulties on account of the many downed telephone poles scattered around, each lying in a pool of its own sawdust.

(((

I've heard that children resemble their fathers at birth for evolutionary reasons. If a father sees himself reflected in his child, he admires her and won't eat her. This feels true because I looked just like Loyd and I often caught him staring at me like I was just about the best thing he ever saw. I was also fierce like him when I was little. Quick to bite. Mom wrote "mad when made to mind" in my baby book and also recorded my first spanking at six months old, for throwing a temper tantrum. Loyd was proud of my ferocity. He'd smile when he said I was *full of piss and vinegar.*

But I was different than Loyd in one very important way. I was a girl. Mom was forever tightening my pigtails and tsk-tsking my grass stains. Like my dad, I was scrawny. Because I was a girl, he interpreted that as fragile. It perplexed him that I would run behind my brother, fall and get back up, strive to keep pace. Jesse skewed me toward the boyish. I was happy to play cars with him, but it was unimaginable that he might play dolls. Jesse taught me to burp my ABCs, double-dog-dared me to eat ants, and beat me thumb wrestling, every time. Our version of uncle always ended with me crying, pacing, and rubbing my knuckles. Still, I'd challenge him to a rematch because I was so pissed at myself for crying uncle.

Loyd wasn't sure what to do with me. He let me into football games, even sometimes chose me to *go long,* but only he was allowed to tackle me. He always warned me before a tackle by yelling out, *timber!* Sometimes, he'd bark out for me to close my legs when I was sitting and he sent me to wash up more often than Jesse. He had trouble letting me be independent. And though he admired my feral side, he got real angry when it crossed his.

Before I learned to be on my best behavior around Loyd, my piss and vinegar caused me trouble. Stomping fits and reckless retaliations always brought pain, but I kept coming back for more. Having a daughter who spit and fought was confusing for Loyd. Maybe that's why he was always teaching me a lesson.

Now honey, it hurt Daddy real bad to do it but I had to teach you a lesson that day you gobbled up all your pudding like an animal. I couldn't have you running around being greedy and selfish.

Nobody can agree if I was three or four that night Mom bought a box of chocolate Jell-O pudding mix for dessert. *Now that was a real treat, Tina Marie, and you were a real pest about it, trying to get your hands into that pudding all damn day.* Jesse and I each poured a cup of milk into the saucepan, but Mom dumped in the powder herself because we fought over it. Standing together on the vinyl seat of a kitchen chair, we took turns stirring, watching it thicken. Mom portioned it into four bowls on a cookie sheet and put it in the fridge for after dinner. I didn't want to eat my real food. Loyd asked why I pushed my peas and carrots to the side of my plate. I said because they were yucky. He gave his standard response for when we weren't happy with the food we were given.

Well, it pushes a turd.

Mom had a simple rule—no vegetables, no pudding. So I forced them down. *By the time your Mama put that pudding in front of you, you were all worked up, squirming in your seat like the Tasmanian devil.* I watched her carry the cookie sheet to the table with such awe you'd think she was the Pope or something. Four milky white Pyrex cereal bowls with brown stripes circling them, each stripe thinner as they fell downward. Mom set one before each of us like we were diners at a fancy restaurant. I put my hands on either side of my cold bowl, brought my nose down to sniff the smooth chocolate surface. Then I went to town.

Your Mama asked you to use your spoon but you weren't having it. Sweetheart, you slurped up that pudding straight from the bowl like a dog. I couldn't just let you ignore your Mama like that. No way, no how.

My pudding was gone in seconds and I asked for more. Loyd thought that was pretty damn funny since I had so much left on my face and in my hair. Once I'd scraped and licked as much as I could off myself, I asked for more again. Mom was patient and explained that we each had the same amount, that next time I should eat more slowly and take time to enjoy my portion. I wasn't listening.

Please can I have more pudding? I tried manners because Mom liked that. She put her spoon down and drew a slow breath, preparing to talk me through a fit. Instead, Loyd spoke up.

You want more pudding, hun?

Yes, yes I did. But I felt cautious. I'd been pestering Mom. I didn't pester my dad if I could help it. I sat up tall and turned to him. I can see us all around the Formica tabletop, feel the pressure build.

You sure you want more pudding?

Yes! I was sure.

This is Daddy's pudding. I'll give it to you, but are you sure you want Daddy's pudding, even though that means Daddy don't get any?

You looked at your Mama like she had the answer. But Daddy asked again.

Tina Marie, do you want my pudding?

Now, saying I remember this incident is a stretch. My memory of it is all wrapped up in the story Loyd told over the years. I'm guessing I looked to my mom because she was my barometer and I had enough sense to know Loyd's pressure was shifting fast. I imagine the air was suddenly still and I felt a twinge of power because everyone was suspended, waiting on me. I had stumbled into collusion with my dad. I was like him, stopping time with my bad behavior.

Mom and Jesse stopped eating to watch Loyd and me like were acting out the final scene in *Hamlet* or something. And I bet it sort of felt good. As I grew, I'd become more aware of this kind of performance. It felt like tennis or dancing, a thing that requires two people understand each other and coordinate. I was looking into his eyes and maybe I didn't know what would happen next but I had confidence in our synchronicity. Throwing a fit had worked and now I was pretty sure I might get more pudding. Or at least that's how I imagine it.

Tina Marie, are you SURE you want Daddy's pudding?

Yes, Daddy! Yes, please.

Well honey, I gave it to ya. And I can promise you one thing, it hurt Daddy a whole lot more than it hurt you.

Loyd stood and walked over to me. I'm sure he didn't seem in a hurry. He knelt down so his face was level with mine, his chest facing me, his right hand between my shoulder blades, left hand on the table, bowl of pudding in his palm. He looked at me like he loved me and I was part of something hilarious. Like he was about to say, *pull my finger.* I bet there was a hint of chuckle in his voice. He was having a hard time holding his laughter before delivering the punch line. Here you go, he said, here's my pudding.

His right hand ran up my neck and held the back of my head firm, his left lifted the bowl and smashed it, softly, into my face. He held me like that a minute, or maybe an hour. Cold chocolate pushed into my nostrils, and it felt like drowning at first. Once I forced it out with air, it was not entirely unpleasant in the bowl. At least I felt hidden and didn't have to see the look on Jesse's face. Plus, there was always a moment of relief, after the worst had happened, when I'd think, *well, I got through that, it wasn't so bad.*

Mom wasn't so sure the worst had happened yet. She gauged her options, placed them on the internal scales she used to balance out her life. Measuring the weight of possible consequences made her calm, still. In those moments, her hesitation had its own tangible energy that filled my chest like held breath. She offered Loyd her pudding, pushing the mostly full bowl toward him.

It's not about the damn pudding. He set his bowl down in front of me.

It's about acting like a selfish little brat. I can see him plop back down in his chair, slap his hand on the table.

Well, I don't think she'll be asking for our pudding again, right Jess? And his warm, tickled laugh broke the tension. Mom's shoulders dropped. She got up and started gathering dishes.

Jesse probably looked at me with a raised eyebrow and I'd understand that to mean I had pushed when I shouldn't have. I usually figured that out just a bit too late. Jesse had a gift for defusing Loyd and he was always patching things up for me.

Jess, you wanna do some wrastlin' before bed? This was how Loyd said "wrestling." It was a common pattern, that after I pushed Loyd and he asserted dominance, he'd invite Jesse to play or give him a treat of some sort. Jesse would give an enthusiastic, *yeah!* I knew I was supposed to watch and feel left out, but I'm pretty sure I finished up Loyd's pudding instead.

Storytelling is powerful. Loyd told that story enough it became my history. He thought it was charming, a silly mishap. Sometimes, he'd ask my mom or brother to tell it, which they'd do but reluctantly and with less spectacle. Just a sentence or two. In Loyd's opinion, it was an appropriate way to teach a toddler not to be selfish, and I didn't think to question that because I knew I'd been wrong to demand more than my fair share.

As I got older, I noticed people seemed uncomfortable when my dad shared that story. Whenever he went too far like that, I imagined it wasn't really him but some monster that took over, like a werewolf. A force that emerged without his consent. Children need their fathers and the wolf allowed me to separate Loyd from his bad behavior. But that got hard to believe when I noticed it was Loyd who kept retelling the story.

(((

Sweetheart, after you just about drowned down there in California, I figured the sooner you learned to swim, the better. Learning to swim is another memory I don't trust. When I set my mind to it, I can feel myself clinging to Loyd in the pool at Sol Duc hot springs. I can hear him complaining that my bony butt is sharp as it rests on his forearm, his left hand fanned out from his body, resting on the surface the way a water skipper does. He tried to ease me off him, asked me to let go, but I was too scared.

As he worked to pry me away, he told me the story of how he almost drowned once while scuba diving. It's a story where he plays the fool, realizes he was afraid for no reason. He was trying to be funny and lighten my mood but it didn't work. I stuck to him like puncture vine, sharp and annoying.

It seems remarkable now, that Loyd ever went scuba diving. It's the sort of thing people with money do. Besides logging, I'd never known him to do much that required special equipment or training he couldn't give himself. Maybe it was snorkeling? Anyway, he said he was diving and got real scared because, even though he loved swimming more than just about anything, he didn't like being that deep. He could feel the weight of all that water above him. The pressure of it. He was just getting his bearings when an octopus attacked him. He lost his head, thrashing around. When he calmed down of course he saw there was no octopus. *I'd got myself tangled in a big ol' patch of seaweed, thick as rope. More I fought, worse I made things. Hear that sweetheart, Daddy almost drowned himself, getting all worked up over nothin'.*

This story never felt true to me. I could picture Loyd in the woods because I'd seen him there more times than I could count. But I couldn't imagine him in a forest of kelp, or even what a forest of kelp might look like. I knew Loyd to swim in lakes, rivers, wide spots in creeks, with his cutoff denim shorts and a blanket thrown out on the bank. But I'd never seen him swim in an ocean. We'd walked the beach together many times, but the sea I knew was too cold for swimming. I'd run from the waves with my dad until I dropped, exhausted, into his arms, but we never went swimming in them.

Plus, the scuba story felt contrived. Like he was making it up to teach me something. That's something he did sometimes, I think. I don't trust myself to know for sure. I'd spend most of my life without my dad. What do I know? Maybe he did go scuba diving and maybe he did think he was gonna drown at the bottom of the sea like that.

What I do know is that the octopus story didn't help when Loyd kept trying to let go of me in the pool. Learning to swim wasn't a gentle experience. Like a terrier follows its nose, Loyd always acted on instinct. He was only gentle when it felt good to him. I was irritating him with my clinging. His failure to get through to me was an insult. He pried me off his hip, attached me to the side of the pool, and swam away.

After leaving me there awhile, he came back. Not close enough to touch, but almost. He started off encouraging.

C'mon honey, you can do it. Just like Daddy showed you. Three strokes and you're here. His arms stretched toward me. Closing most of the space between us. I didn't move.

Daddy won't let you sink, I promise. When that didn't work, he started to get mad.

Tina Marie, you ain't getting outta this water until you swim to me. Then he tried playing on my empathy.

You think Daddy would let you drown? That hurts Daddy's feelings. He even tried involving Jesse, but still, I wouldn't let go of the wall. My sense of self-preservation was too strong. If I set off toward him I wouldn't make it, I knew that. And I wasn't sure he'd save me. I don't think this is symbolic of our relationship or anything. Plenty of kids with perfectly stable dads feel the same way. He could tell I wasn't confident in him and that pissed him off. Loyd was most sure of his love for us when he was angry—that's how he could justify his actions.

Along with the scuba story, Loyd kept bringing up the time he saved me from drowning. It was a concrete reminder of why he had to push me so hard. He thought the drowning story should motivate me to swim. Instead, it motivated me to cling to safety. Finally, I wore him out. Tired of my acting like a baby, he pulled me out of the water and held me. I thought it was over and I think he knew that. Sometimes, this was the worst part about my dad, how he'd sense vulnerability and take advantage of it. I felt the sun warming my whole body and melted into his arms. I'm sure he felt my muscles go slack, my grip loosen, before he threw me in.

Now honey, I know it sounds mean but I watched you drown once and I wasn't gonna let it happen again. And I promise you it was about the hardest thing Daddy ever did, throwing you in like that. But it's my job, making sure you can swim, and I'll be damned if I'm not gonna do my job.

I probably don't need to tell you how that went. Cruel or not, it's a timeless way to teach children to swim. I sputtered, choked, and sank. Loyd pulled me out when I really seemed in trouble, gave me a few moments and some quick encouragement, threw me back in. Again and again until I managed a desperate doggy paddle. He let me take a break then and I worked really hard to seem injured and not show my pride. I didn't want to reward his method. But I was glad when he said we weren't leaving until he saw me do it again.

This time I climbed down the ladder myself. I decided when to let go. My own scrawny arms and legs managed to keep me up and even propel me forward. Loyd whooped and hollered and cannon balled in right next to me. I wasn't annoyed at being splashed and that was out of character. He circled me, his waves pushing inward, and made a big deal of my breakthrough. Loyd was an excellent swimmer. He favored the freestyle stroke, but I don't think he knew that's what it's called. When he tried to teach it to me, he called it *swimming overhand.*

Loyd might not have the proper terms down, but I've seen few people with better form. Because Loyd didn't just have good form; he had what I can only call natural expression, like a musician who's technically skilled but also has an intrinsic feel for music. When Loyd was swimming I swear even the water was enjoying itself. Swimming is work and Loyd loved work. Unlike regular work, he was weightless when swimming. Being light like that is its own sort of happiness.

That day, I felt that weightless joy for the first time. Though I tried to hide it from Loyd, I'm pretty sure it shined through. And I guess I'm a sucker for work, too, since my wild strokes were making it way more work than it had to be. I kept at my clumsy dog paddle while Loyd relaxed into an easy backstroke, orbiting me wherever I went and speaking much louder than he needed to.

I've never really mastered swimming. Like my dad, I love to swim in natural bodies of water. On a hot day, I might feel the call and drive an hour or more to jump in a lake. But I'm still pretty pathetic as far as form goes. I can backstroke and breaststroke all right, but my freestyle feels fake or forced. I'm always worried somebody who knows about swimming will see me and think I'm an idiot. When I do try swimming overhand, I like to imagine Loyd, pushing through the water in his cutoffs, tattered fringe chasing behind him in a graceful drift. When I do that, it feels like I'm saying to the water, *remember Loyd? I'm his daughter, can't you tell?* My childhood fears of carnivorous fish and drowning in endless dark caverns somehow evolved into a desire to immerse myself in bodies of water full of unknown elements, bottoms I can't see. I've come to love floating in all that possibility. Loyd had something to do with that.

(((

We lived in so many little mill towns in my first five years. Randle, Packwood, Morton, Sekiu, Sandpoint, Headquarters, Oroville, and more. We lived in trailers, cabins, one-room studios, more trailers. Mom finally convinced Loyd to settle down in Clallam Bay, Washington, before Jesse started first grade. Crown Zellerbach was the second-largest lumber company shaving the surface of the Pacific Northwest back then and Loyd was lucky enough to get on their payroll. He was proud to be a company man, though it wouldn't last. For many years, I'd feel that pride linger a moment whenever I saw a white metal Crown Zellerbach paper towel dispenser in a public bathroom.

When we first got to Clallam Bay, we lived in the Mansion. Before long, we sold it and rented a big double-wide in a trailer park on a bluff looking down on the ocean. This was the kind of trailer that actually needs some furniture. It wasn't all built in. Sometimes, when Mom wanted to make dinner in peace or go to the Laundromat alone, Loyd would say, *you kids wanna go on a wander?* He meant a walk on the beach. There was never a time we didn't want to go. I could have a bellyache and a fever and I'd still go on a wander. We'd walk on that beach with Loyd as long as he'd let us, no matter how cold our faces or fierce the wind. I had a powder-blue pea coat with polyester white fur lining that I thought was so pretty, though it had belonged to another girl before me. It wasn't even a little bit water resistant but I didn't care. You know how sometimes you're listening to a song you love and all you can think about is restarting that same song as soon as it's over? That's what it was like to walk on the beach with my dad.

Loyd stopped often to stoop down and point things out along the shore. He'd gather seashells or bits of interesting flotsam. Not just gather— consider. He might hold up a piece of broken shell and ask, *what's that look like to you, hun?* He was truly interested in my interpretation. He'd ask if I could imagine it as the head, foot, or body of one of his seashell creatures. He used a hot glue gun to put together shells and create silly figures, some on two legs, some on four, six, or eight. He'd add plastic googly eyes then take them down to a tourist shop and sell them. Our beach walks were collecting missions to gather shells, driftwood, moss, and rocks for his critters.

But it was about more than collecting. Loyd would hold up a piece of driftwood and ask us to look at the way the sea had shaped it. We discovered mermaids, dragons, wiener dogs. Driftwood can be anything and Loyd never got tired of that idea. It's just plain wood but also a tadpole, a giant's pointer finger, a long, skinny Ford pickup truck. He taught us to compare today's landscape with yesterday's, to observe the way the ocean kept on changing the lines of our walking. Nothing's stronger than the power of the sea. Nothing's got more slow patience. Not the coastline with its craggy bluffs, not the mountains or the rivers or even the forest.

I lived in a small body then and when Loyd knelt down to talk to me, to show me the miracle of an unbroken sand dollar or newly forming inlet, he looked like a man at prayer. What I mean to say is that he made me feel like I deserved to take up space. From his moments of careful attention, I learned to expect some amount of worship from the world. From his violence, desperate apologies, and absences, I would discover that the same sparkling fires that fueled his creativity could burn out of control, leaving a landscape stripped of life. Loyd would hurt and fail me in a hundred ways, but first he taught me to wonder, gave me love without condition, and moments where I felt holy.

rough house

OUR LIFE IN THE WOODS couldn't last forever. Our family always had the feel of something temporary. Mom says living in trailers was like living in a tin can firetrap. I'm pretty sure she's picturing a soup can when she says that but it always made me think of the hissing release of pressure I'd hear when I opened up a Shasta cola. Even that new double-wide was just too small for the four of us. As Jesse and I grew older and more independent, it was harder for Mom to keep us out of Loyd's way. I don't know if he got angry more often the older we got, or if we just noticed more.

Jesse started school in Clallam Bay and Mom signed him up for Cub Scouts and T-ball. Before long she was his den mother and had some friends. It started to feel permanent. Loyd knew enough to be grateful for steady work with Crown Zellerbach but I think the monotony was hard on him. He was feral at heart and migration suited him. He itched to move and this caused little eruptions. He'd binge, disappearing for a night and coming back wrecked. He'd sometimes spend recklessly, buying something extravagant we didn't need, though the bills weren't paid.

One payday, Loyd came home with a brand-new Atari. You'd have thought he'd won the lottery, he was so tickled. And we did feel rich. The Atari was meant to delight Jesse, and it did. But we were all surprised at how much Mom came to love that thing. She was suspicious of it at first, worried about money. Before long she became the Pac-Man champ of the family. Watching her and Jesse play together was more fun than actually playing. Mom would move her entire body along with her little yellow character, hollering to make it go faster, leaning into corners, and jumping out of her seat when a ghost chomped her up.

Dad also bought a handgun off another logger in his outfit. Mom was less happy with this splurge. She'd been waiting for payday so she could pay for Jesse's Cub Scout uniform and Loyd knew it. This was just the sort of thing he'd do to flex his muscle, show Mom who wore the pants. His buddy was hard up for cash and needed to sell his gun, *and I'll be goddamned if I'm not gonna help out a buddy.*

One day Loyd came home from work with a shoulder sore from cutting old-growth Doug firs with trunks wide enough to be kitchen tables. He'd pulled a muscle or something but he *wasn't about to go to no doctor.* Mom was waiting on him, hoping he'd be in a good mood and willing to keep an eye on us so she could run to the store alone. She could tell by the way he fought with the flimsy aluminum screen door that she'd be hauling us along with her to get the shopping done. So she packed us up and headed out for bread and milk.

Loyd hollered out the door after us. Hun, get me a tube of Ben-Gay for this damn shoulder. She told him she didn't have enough money. There was just enough for bread and milk. Well, Loyd said, if I don't work, we don't eat and if I don't get Ben-Gay, I don't work. She asked if he had any money. He said no.

At the market, Mom reached to grab a tube of Ben-Gay and found a twenty-dollar bill behind it. In that moment, she started to think maybe the Lord was watching out for her. She bought a gallon of milk, bread, bologna, and Cream of Wheat. She felt like a hero walking in the door that night. Loyd had been self-medicating while we were gone and couldn't be convinced that she'd just found twenty bucks. He figured she'd been hiding money. Loyd worked himself into a tizzy so Mom sent us off to bed early, because his shoulder wasn't too hurt to express his anger.

Even so, the feeling Mom got when she found that money, of being blessed or watched over by God, stuck with her. It felt like a message, assurance from outside her own head that she and her kids deserved milk and bread. God showed his people their birthright when he sent manna down from heaven. God also led his people out of Egypt. With that twenty dollars Mom started to think maybe she was being led somewhere, too.

Mom always kept the change from groceries and errands in a bowl on the kitchen counter. It was an unspoken rule that money belonged to Loyd. The bowl allowed him to see how much money Mom had at her disposal. But the change from the Ben-Gay twenty was not Loyd's. Mom split it up and stashed it around the trailer in places where it could seem like a simple mistake. A coat pocket, the bottom of her purse, our piggy banks, and her heart-shaped metal jewelry box with the romantic scene of Victorian lovers set into the lid. She kept her change hidden away and it grew in the dark. She started paying more attention, skimming from the regular change bowl, leftovers from trips to the gas station, the post office, and the market. She wasn't even sure why she did it at first. She just knew it felt good to have her own money and it felt right because it all started with that twenty from God.

Though we were settled like Mom had wanted, she started to imagine another life. It wasn't just the Ben-Gay money that started her thinking she'd had enough of Loyd's drinking, drugging, cheating, and hitting. Mom felt a new sort of shame for her life. Though we never asked it out loud, she could see the question in our maturing faces. Why did she keep letting Daddy hit her? She'd also had an experience a few years before that started to gnaw at her mind again.

In our migrating years, Mom often babysat for other families. Loyd didn't want her taking money so she'd usually do it for trade. One family fell apart during that time, the wife leaving her heavy-fisted husband in an act of bravery many timber wives imagined but few achieved. Mom would babysit for the newly single mother while Loyd was at work and wouldn't know she was helping the woman out. Her son was Jesse's age. One day, Mom sent both boys out to play while she made lunch. A short chain-link fence circled the small patch of grass beside our trailer. When Mom called the boys in to eat, Jesse's little friend was gone. When Mom asked where he went, Jesse said his daddy came and got him.

The boys hadn't known to be afraid of a daddy. When the man came to the fence, the little boy was happy to see him. The man reached over, picked up his son, and walked away. When we moved on a few months later, the mother still hadn't found her son and Mom doesn't know if she ever did. She felt awful that the boy was taken on her watch, but it haunted her for another reason. It felt like a threat. This is what happens when a woman gets ideas about independence.

(((

On a warm night at the end of summer, Loyd was late coming home from work. We'd finished dinner and it was almost time to get ready for bed when he showed up, shit-faced. As soon as Mom saw his dark eyes, she told us to go get in our PJs and brush our teeth. We resisted. Not to be brats or avoid bedtime, but because we knew she was trying to remove us and we'd developed an urge to protect her. There's an awakening that happens for children who live in violence and ours had begun. I can see now that Jesse's had started long before.

Jesseandtina, I said go get ready for bed. We knew she meant business when she stuck our names together like that. We walked back to our room to change.

When I stand outside that trailer now and look in at this scene, I like to imagine that we chose our Underoos for pajamas that night. Underoos were these superhero-themed underwear sets for children that came with a top and a bottom. We each had one precious set. Jesse had Spider-Man and I had Wonder Woman. They were underwear, not sleepwear, but we liked to sleep in them because then at least we could see them. Seemed stupid to us that we'd hide them under our clothes during the day. In my earliest memory of admiring my body in a mirror, I'm wearing my Wonder Woman Underoos. I had to get up on the edge of the bathtub to stand tall in the mirror and admire the red tank top with a yellow eagle merging into a W shape against my puffed-out chest, the dark blue underwear covered in white stars. Thing is, my Underoos made me feel strong. When I look back at those children now, I want to give them armor. So I dress them as superheroes.

Mom offered Loyd dinner, started heating up a can of tomato soup and grilling a cheese sandwich. Handed him water in a tall aluminum cup. She talked calm, but not too calm. Loyd felt guilty about going out. And things got ugly when Loyd mixed guilt with drugs and alcohol. Mom tried to shrink. Sometimes that worked. This time, it just created space for the monster to get through.

We saw the transition. The wolf, the monster, whatever you want to call it—Loyd was under its control. He went to the closet and got out the handgun he'd bought from his buddy. Said he was gonna clean it, but that didn't explain why he pulled out the box of bullets, too. He set the gun and the box of bullets on the table by the couch and sat down. Mom told us it was time to hop in bed, her voice false and chirpy.

I'll come tuck you in soon.

Again we were reluctant but complied, faster this time. We went to hug each of them goodnight. We knew it was our job to act as if nothing was wrong. Usually, Loyd allowed her to send us to bed so they could hash things out. This time, he wasn't about to let her take charge. I hugged and kissed him goodnight and stepped away so Jesse could have his turn. Except Jesse didn't follow me. Loyd didn't release him. He rotated Jesse to face Mom, draped his left arm across Jesse's upper chest, and settled his right hand on my brother's little forehead, just under the tenacious cowlick above Jesse's left eye. Mom kept trying to tame that stubborn bit of hair but it always won. Jesse's back was against Loyd's chest, one of the safest places he knew. But we all understood he wasn't safe, that Loyd's hold was a threat. In his seven years Jesse had never been on the receiving end of Loyd's violence.

Mom told me to go to our room and stay there. The gun sat on the table, urging me not to move. She repeated her command. I heard the begging in her voice and turned away. But I hid in the narrow hall because I felt sure I could keep my brother safe if I could keep my eyes on him. We always went to our room together. We always listened to the shuffling on the other side of the wall, the whimpering and grunting. The smacking sound that reminded me of Mom tenderizing meat with her wooden mallet. We heard it all together and we tried to imagine origins for those sounds that we could live with. I couldn't do that alone. So I crouched down against the wood-paneled wall, below the "God, Grant Me the Serenity" prayer. It was printed in fancy brown cursive on parchment-looking paper. A border around the whole thing was meant to make it look like a scroll unfurling. It was fastened to the wall with flat, silver thumbtacks.

It felt like hours but could've been minutes that I waited in the hall. A couple of times I woke, my chin hitting my chest. The moon made her slow patrol across the sky and gravity followed. Loyd's wave started to ebb so he released my brother. Mom sent Jesse to bed. I stood as he walked quietly to the hall. I didn't want him to see me slumped on the floor and sleepy. I wanted to be a sister who stayed alert until he was safe, wanted him to know that mattered to me even though I'd been unable to actually do it.

We went to our room and climbed in bed together. We didn't say anything about it and we never have. I wish I could say we stayed awake, tried to will our mother's safety. But we were exhausted. Our bodies wrung dry of tears and sweat and the energy spent paying attention to Loyd. I get a little repulsed when adults celebrate the resilience of children. We weren't resilient. We were depleted and our bodies knew the need to rest for another day, another challenge.

I think we tell ourselves children are resilient because it relieves us of worry about the trauma they endure. But there is no trauma that doesn't wound and I don't know that injury can fully heal. Nothing that's broken can ever be whole like it was before breaking. Maybe our focus on resilience teaches children the wrong lesson. Maybe instead of fooling ourselves that our children will heal, that they'll be restored or cleaned of their traumas, we should teach them to find beauty in their scars.

Releasing Jesse must've felt like a loss to Loyd, like compromise. From the sound of things he got worked up all over again. Still, we drifted off.

Mom was grateful we did fall asleep because Loyd eventually pushed his way into our room and this time the gun was in his hand. He touched the gun to Jesse's sweaty head and held it there while Mom begged and cried. I can imagine the fine shimmer of sweat across Jesse's forehead, the way his eyelashes looked so long when he slept. I sometimes used to wake up during fights. I'd pretend to be asleep and listen. I don't want that for Jesse on this night. I want him to sleep and grow up without ever knowing Loyd did this.

There was an exhausting negotiation and rehashing of old feelings that resurfaced when the wolf came around. Eventually Loyd lowered the gun and walked back out to the living room. He was still on edge. She talked him into unloading the gun but he wouldn't hand it over. He did give her the ammunition. She picked up the box and replaced the bullets, counting as she restored it to a full box. She got up and walked across the room, talking calm at him. When she got near the door, she pulled it open and bolted out.

She ran into the night, a bird drawing the predator away from her nest. It worked. The wolf was always more interested in hurting Mom than us. Using us was just a way to control her. By running, she'd removed us from his range, but reignited his rage. She knew it would hurt if he caught her. The fact that he had to be so quiet, outside among the other trailers well past bedtime, only made him more angry.

She hoped, if she could keep the bullets from him until he exhausted himself, he might pass out and be sorry in the morning. She knew Loyd didn't want to hurt any of us. She also knew that gun gave the wolf power to do sudden and irreparable damage that Loyd didn't intend. One of my aunts, who had two and a half fingers missing from her right hand, was living with the consequences of loving a man with guns and a substance problem.

Mom ran between trailers, ducking down to rest near the hitches. She could feel him getting closer. She dropped to the ground and crawled under a fifth wheel to hide. He got frustrated looking for her. Soon he got the idea and started dropping to his knees to look underneath each trailer as he passed. When he was only one row away, she stashed the ammo box up into the bowels of the trailer and then, wrapping her arms and legs around whatever she could get ahold of, pulled herself up against the greasy undercarriage. She suspended herself like that long after he passed.

Even when she lowered herself to the ground, she stayed under that trailer. She laid there after she stopped hearing his boots in the dusty gravel. Crunch, crunch, pause, Crunch, crunch, pause. Until after the crickets started singing again and she could see the light of the moon instead of just her own fear. She heard him open and close the trailer door, slowly, quietly. That was a good sign, the slowing down. Loyd's physical presence turned just plain sorry when he came down from an episode like this. His posture, the sounds he made, embodied shame. She waited what felt like hours, then pulled herself out and crept back inside. Jesse and I were in our bed, chests rising and falling. Loyd was passed out on their bed, still fully dressed, on top of the blankets. She hid the gun in one spot, the bullets in another. She took his boots off and got in beside him.

In the morning he was so sorry. Mom told him she wouldn't live that way. She'd grown up with that bullshit and she wasn't about to have her kids live with it. He said all the right things. She was right (again). She shouldn't have to live that way (again). Tears and promises (again), he couldn't believe himself (again), he was gonna quit (again), he'd never hurt her (again), or the kids (again). He'd find an AA meeting right after work, promise. He gave her extra grocery money and told her she should take us to ice cream.

Late that afternoon, we ran to the post office to mail a letter to my aunt Ruth. On our way home, Mom saw Loyd's pickup in front of the tavern. She pulled in, parked, told us to stay in the car. Just before she got out, she took a long breath, her shoulders rising, chest filling. I think going into that bar might've been the hardest thing she did that day, because she knew there was no going back if she saw him in there. Still, she had to be sure. She walked in and there was Loyd. He smiled at her, that irresistible twinkle in his eyes, the cheerful Loyd who only existed for a few beers. She mourned a little, I think, looking at his eyes right then.

Hey Hun, he said, I won a bet with Doug so the sorry sonofabitch owed me one. He had a partial in front of him, another already lined up. Several empty shot glasses between them.

She told him she'd seen his truck and figured she better stop and let him know dinner would be late. Our errands had run long. She had a couple more stops, then she'd get home and start dinner, but he could take his time.

Mom drove straight home and started moving around the trailer, gathering up all her stashed money. Then she collected clothes, towels, sheets, packing them inside pillowcases. She put the Atari in a laundry basket. Jesse and I helped, carrying small bundles out to the car. She was rushed, quiet, and meticulous. She'd imagined it all, knew what to grab and how to pack it efficiently. I felt her need for silence and compliance. She didn't ask, we just knew. Her trips from car to trailer were calm and manic at the same time. There was an economy in her anxiety, her arms always full, her selections careful. She told us to put on the pajamas she'd set out and to gather some toys for a long car ride. We changed and waited for her in the living room while she finished packing. She came back in one last time, looked around, picked me up, and carried me to the car, Jesse trailing behind her.

She set me down on a bed of blankets and towels lining the backseat of her Ford Fiesta. A soft blue blanket covered the layers folded under me. She'd put the pillow from my bed there so I could rest my head when I got tired. Jesse sat up front on a similar perch. The hatchback behind me was packed with stuffed pillowcases, shoes, a mixing bowl full of Tupperware, pots and pans nested together, the smallest filled with silverware. A laundry basket with cereal, pasta, flour, sugar, and cans of soup. Another filled with soap, shampoo, aspirin, Band-Aids, and toilet paper. At my feet was a paper sack with saltine crackers, a loaf of bread, peanut butter, and a butter knife.

We drove away from Loyd and for the first time I felt the solid lump of separation grow in my throat. Mom said we were going to visit Aunt Ruth in Oregon but I'm pretty sure Jesse and I knew better. Half of me wanted to run back to my daddy, half of me was afraid he'd follow us. I imagined

Loyd coming home that night and finding us gone. Would he yell or cry? I pictured him at the gas station pay phone, calling around to Mom's friends and sisters to see if anyone knew where we were.

Whatever he did, it wouldn't matter. Nobody in the whole world knew where we were, except for Mom. We could've driven off a cliff into the sea and no one would know. There's a particular sort of isolation that can erupt, like a chemical reaction, out of poverty. People disappear.

In some ways, we did disappear that night. The people we used to be were gone. We transformed into different children, Mom into a different woman. She would work and we would be latchkey kids. No more wandering walks, no more woods or whittling. My time with Loyd had always been ongoing. Now, it would be like TV episodes, each with a beginning and end. And all the time in between episodes would be acts of imagination. I'd live mostly with Mom in this world full of danger she was constantly trying to protect me from. Being with Loyd was different. He was strong enough to keep me safe from outside threats but couldn't always protect me from himself.

I fell asleep for most of the seven-hour drive. Mom woke us in the dark and made us go into a cold rest-stop bathroom with her. I said I didn't have to go but she said just try and she was right. When we climbed back into the car she locked the doors and took a nap, leaving the keys in the ignition. After some rest, we all tried to pee again before moving on.

(((

I don't remember Loyd telling us folk stories, but I associate tall tales with my dad. The adventures of Paul Bunyan and Babe the Blue Ox are worked into the folds of my childhood like the nicotine soaked up in the wood-panel walls of that rented double-wide in Clallam Bay. My earliest experiences of empathy are wrapped up in those stories, the feeling of sadness that settled over me at the thought of the giant lumberjack and his trusty sidekick. Tall tales are supposed to be funny, but I couldn't get over the way Paul's neighbors cast him out or the fact he outlives Babe. To this day I can't think of Paul Bunyan without picturing him standing over Babe, who

I always insisted was a girl ox, lying in the huge grave he dug for her in the Black Hills.

Paul Bunyan was so enormous that, when he was just a baby, he rolled over in his sleep and caused an earthquake. He was so fast he could shut out the light and jump in bed before his room even got dark. I was always trying it myself, though I admit my hurry had more to do with fear that something might grab me in the dark. Remarkable people are often doomed to be lonely. Because of the troubles his size caused, Paul's neighbors didn't want to live near him. Loyd was like Paul in this way—it was dangerous to be too close to him.

Because he was rejected, Paul built himself a logging camp and lived alone in the woods. One winter day, he came across a scrawny baby ox abandoned in the snow. He took the little calf home and sat her by the fire and even though she got warm and fluffy, the blue of that cold night stayed with her. Babe the Blue Ox had been cast out because she was a runt but Paul's love made her grow huge in proportion to him. Babe helped Paul with all sorts of logging jobs, the two of them often helping the very people who'd rejected them. Paul could tie the end of a twisty logging road to Babe's tail and she'd yank that road straight. If there was a logjam on the river, Babe could jump in and swish her tail to break it loose.

Loyd was always building structures and rigging up contraptions and this also reminded me of Paul Bunyan. According to old-timers, Paul had a huge kitchen in Oregon. All his helpers were regular-sized men, which made their work interesting in such an enormous kitchen. His stove was an acre wide and as tall as a grandaddy pine. Servers had to be hoisted up onto the table with pulleys and they rode bicycles to get from one end to the other. They skated over the stovetop with pork fat tied to their boots to grease the griddle for Paul's massive pancakes. One time, Babe accidently knocked over a giant sack of dried peas with her tail. Most of them flew up into the sky and landed in a nearby hot spring. Paul's crew ate nothing but pea soup for months after that.

Even though Paul filled his camp with loggers, he never had a truer friend than Babe. Together, they worked faster than any other crew since

Paul could take down a whole stand of trees with one swipe of his ax and Babe could haul all the logs out in a single trip. Paul dug the Great Lakes just so Babe could always find a drink of water. When she died he dug her a grave three miles wide. Or was it five?

I always thought there was a good chance those stories were true. Unlike fairy tales and princess stories full of magic impossibilities, Paul Bunyan felt practical and realistic. Like Loyd, Paul was a logger. He wore suspenders over flannel shirts and hefted an ax on his shoulder in a posture as familiar to me as my father's voice. Paul was a hard-working man who ate pancakes and enjoyed a good laugh. The greatest magic he knew was the companionship of a true friend. His size alienated him from his community but it also made him valuable. Like Loyd, he was stronger than most and could accomplish tasks that seemed impossible. Like Loyd, he often destroyed things by an accident of his nature.

Eventually Babe died and left Paul alone. Everyone knows animals tend to live shorter lives than men. When Babe let out her final breath there was no fairy godmother to revive her. Paul had to be lonely, simple as that. This isolation, too, reflected Loyd's life. Sometimes living means you have to be lonely, you just have to sit with it. Maybe that's why those stories still sit with me, there is nothing more true to me than the image of the isolated lumberman sitting next to his fire at night and missing a love he can never have back.

《 《 《

Aunt Ruth lived on the eastern edge of the Columbia River Gorge, just where the temperate green forest transitions to desert. The Dalles was not a timber town. It was an aluminum town. Mom said we were almost there and I saw twin columns of black smoke marching constantly, with the diligence of an ant colony, from smelter to sky. I'd eventually learn to navigate by those smoke stacks. Until the plant would begin a slow, agonizing decline. Each new wave of layoffs creating another batch of jobless fathers, more kids joining me in the free and reduced lunch line. The Dalles was the first town I'd known to have more than one school, and though it only boasted about eleven thousand people, Loyd would come to call it *The Big City*.

We made it to Aunt Ruth's early in the morning. She was crammed into a two-bedroom apartment with her kids but she took us in. After a while, Mom went down to the courthouse to file for divorce only to learn that Loyd already had. And he had a lawyer.

Mom got a restraining order but that didn't stop Loyd. Once she responded to his divorce petition he knew where we were. He dug up some old mail to get Aunt Ruth's street address and had a buddy drive him to The Dalles. Loyd's name was on the title to Mom's car. So he showed up with the police to take back his stolen property, leaving us to walk everywhere. Mom could tell the officer felt real bad about it, thought Loyd was a grade-A asshole. But the law was on his side.

Because Loyd filed for divorce in Washington, Mom had to go back to appear in court. He thought he was smart, taking her car away so she couldn't get there. But Mom had met a nice older gentleman at the Eagles lodge who took a fancy to her. He loaned her a car and she left us in Oregon while she drove the seven hours back to Clallam County. She had records from her clinic visits, evidence of injuries Loyd had given her. Add that to his arrest record and Loyd wasn't the picture of an ideal parent. Mom was granted sole custody and child support but Loyd never paid it. He said he'd be happy to support us if we came home. *But I ain't about to bankroll your Mama's new life in the Big City.*

When we left Loyd, we left our green life. Evergreen trees large enough to become lumber had looked down on me for as long as memory. Rich, loamy forests cooled hot days. The smell of sawdust had been home. Gasoline and pitch forever soaked into my daddy's clothes and mixed with cigarette and campfire smoke to create his particular scent. In Clallam Bay, wet salt was in the air and moss grew on the rocks. Everything looked soft.

Now we'd have a brown life at the edge of the dry Oregon desert. I looked around for trees and found mostly Ponderosa pine and scrub oaks, their leaves hard and crunchy when they fell. The wide Columbia River rolls slow and steady alongside town, its current invisible. It was once a

fierce and raging river, rich in salmon and famous for the dramatic Cel-
ilo Falls, where ancient people pulled plenty from the river to feed their
families. Now the massive concrete profile of The Dalles Dam blocks the
river, creating depth that drowned the falls. An American flag as big as a
manufactured home is stretched across the dam's wide grey expanse, like a
monument to all we've stolen.

I'd never known a river so wide and wondered why it couldn't manage to make the land it touched feel wet. The hills across the river, built
of soil picked up by wind and piled up on basalt columns, are only green
in early spring. By late April they turn brown and stay that way until snow
covers them. The coast is over a hundred miles away but the sea pushes air
through the gorge, making it perpetually windy. It was easy to imagine I
might dry up and blow away.

Mom was hot sun in dry blue skies so the arid landscape suited her.
She often reminded us that she was a California girl. If she had a day off
in summer, she'd lay out on a blanket, her book and cigarettes beside her,
baby oil shining on her skin. A lizard gathering sun. Loyd was deep, shady
forest and cold, wet coastline. He was the smell of cedar, smoke, and sweat.
I think of him when I walk on a path spongy with pine needles, when I
hear the chatter of woodland creatures, cross a mountain stream, or zip my
collar up against the cold spray of the Pacific.

meetings

JESSE AND I STOOD looking up at an abandoned brick building with boarded windows. I put my sweaty hand in his. I just wanted to get this over with. It was October 1981 and I'd just started kindergarten at Joseph G. Wilson Elementary School. Jesse was in second grade and the kids in his class made it clear that surviving the annual haunted house was a rite of passage. Mom walked us toward the entrance, blocked by a smiling wicked witch waiting to take our tickets.

Mom and Jesse acted like this was a treat, like I should look forward to it. I could tell by the way the hulking red building stood over me that this was not a privilege. But I also knew that sometimes, it's the fate of children to suffer their parent's gifts. This was one of those times and I resolved to smile at Mom as she nudged me along this path of nightmares.

Jesse, keep an eye on your sister. She might get pretty scared in there.

I'd considered faking sick. Turns out it wouldn't be so fake. Nausea bloomed through my belly as soon as I heard the faint creepy soundtrack oozing through the door. Besides, there was no way Mom would send Jesse alone. The moment we left Loyd, making her a single mom, she became vigilant about equality. Our family had a new shape and that meant new rules. Always stick together and always share.

Before, this would've been something Jesse did with Loyd. I wouldn't have to go, though Loyd would badger me to try. Jesse had done that this time. He told me any blood I might see was just ketchup and that I didn't need to be afraid of the monsters because they were just other kids' dads in costume. This wasn't comforting. I already knew dads could be monsters. And I never did see the point in fun you had to be convinced to have. But I knew all about doing things you don't like for the people you love.

This was the kind of thing Loyd loved. He always stopped at roadside attractions, pulled over to take our picture by the Yard Birds mascot, and took us to carnivals and fairs. Because I once threw up in his lap after he convinced me to try a ride called The Hammer Head, Loyd stopped pressuring me to go on rides. I stood behind many temporary safety fences and watched him and Jesse board roller coasters and scramblers. But he always brought me along and I was expected to join them in the funhouse, mirror maze, and whatnot. Said he didn't want me to regret missing out.

Jesse played Loyd's role now, tugging me along into this haunted house. But once the door shut behind us, he seemed afraid. He tightened his grip on my hand, set his chin, and started walking. I kept my left hand in his but twisted my body until I was pretty much facing backwards. I figured this whole thing would be less scary if I could see monsters approach us from behind. And they did.

We survived a mummy, who emerged from his sarcophagus and lurched toward us as we passed. Dr. Frankenstein hardly noticed us. He was focused on his green creature, strapped to a plywood worktable with jumper cables clamped to his ragged sleeves. An elegant vampire in a real wooden coffin woke as we approached, his eyes and sharp teeth daring us to continue. I'm not sure Jesse even noticed—he kept his pace steady and navigated with intent. The last room was a graveyard, a few zombies stumbling toward us. Jesse walked as quickly as he respectably could. The nearest zombie saw the bald terror in my face and gave a gesture that made them all fall back.

Finally, we arrived at a door with a piece of butcher paper taped up, the word *exit* painted on in sloppy red, allowed to drip for dramatic effect. A lady in a black and white maid's uniform guarded the door. Her face was white, poorly applied blood dripping from the corners of her mouth. Her face paint was faded, like maybe she worked a double shift or something. She held us up, waiting for the signal it was our turn to pass. I let go of Jesse's hand and put my back flat against his, facing the way we'd come so none of the monsters could sneak up on us. I was not too proud to be cautious. The creepy maid sensed my anxiety and dropped her scary cackle to make small talk with us in a normal voice. Soon enough she let us through the door but she seemed unsure about it.

The door opened to a plain warehouse. Smooth concrete floors under a tall ceiling with exposed beams, the faint smell of motor oil. It was empty except for some large cardboard boxes sitting around. They were big, like washer or dryer or refrigerator boxes. This almost broke the spell. If this space was used for something so mundane as appliance storage it seemed unlikely it was actually haunted. Plus the maid lady had already started to dissolve the whole aura for me. Still, I wasn't an idiot. I knew better than to relax until I was safely out of the whole building. At the far end from us was a big roll-up door, like on a garage, and it was wide open. Fall sunshine and the silhouette of Mom, waiting for us on the outside.

Seeing my mom standing there was catalyst for two very strong conflicting impulses. I wanted to run to her, no matter how desperate it looked. But I also wanted to be strong, brave, and calm for her. Released from my grip, Jesse walked with slow determination toward the exit. Without him tugging me along, I was frozen between my warring instincts. I pulled my shit together and started walking as steady as I could. I'm sure Mom wasn't buying it. Basically, I was speed walking. Like when you're at school and you waited too long to pee but you're only allowed to walk in the hallway to get to the bathroom. I kept my eyes fixed on Mom, fighting the urge to look behind. Just when I felt I had this under control, the cardboard boxes sprouted human arms and started moving toward us.

The way the boxes ambled might've looked funny to an adult. To my child self it just looked like terror. The air was leaking out of the space between the box monsters and me. The closer they got, the less I could breathe. I felt myself pee a little, which was disappointing. Being the baby was my constant source of shame. I abandoned calm and just ran, balls out, toward the light. Jesse was ahead when a box monster got close enough to touch me, a hand reaching out to brush my shoulder. I screamed and pivoted away, losing one of my black flats. I left the shoe and ran the last stretch, threw my arms around Mom and cried, snotty, panic tears soaking into her jacket. Jesse looked smug, having arrived at her side without any nonsense.

The boxes stopped moving, arms retracting as they settled back down on the concrete. It was like they fed on the fear of children, required it to live. We stood there, looking in at the lifeless boxes surrounding my shoe. Afternoon sun streamed into the warehouse but the shoe was just beyond it, in cold shadow. Mom couldn't afford to buy me new shoes. After a moment she broke the silence.

Jesse, go get your sister's shoe. And he did.

((((

Mom and Loyd were quick to replace each other. She still admits that she was a fool for my daddy. Says he was probably the love of her life and she'd have stayed with him if it wasn't for us kids. She could tolerate the hitting. Leaving Loyd is just one of the million ways Mom made a bridge of her body so her kids could walk across to a better life.

It took a lot for her to leave and she wasn't sure she'd be able to stay away unless there was a new man. We left Loyd in June and by the end of August we were living with Dan. We had to move in with Dan sooner than Mom would've liked. Aunt Ruth's landlord figured out she had an extra three people living in her apartment and kicked us out. Our only other option was Mom's parents. Grandma Thelma offered us the extra room in their trailer up on top of Cherry Heights Road but Mom said no, thank you. Pothead couldn't be trusted around little girls.

When she'd started working, Mom sometimes left us with Grandma. Mom's shifts were mostly while Pothead was gone during the day but still, she'd had a talk with me about private parts, what was OK to touch and whatnot. Mom told it to me straight—said I shouldn't be alone with Grandpa and didn't have to hug him or kiss him or sit on his lap. Same goes for Uncle Johnny or any other adult, for that matter. Mom said I'd just know when something didn't feel right and that was true. I already got a scared feeling from Pothead.

So we moved in with Dan. He was a Vietnam vet and worked rotating shifts at Martin Marietta Aluminum. Mom was stronger now, and Dan was happy to let her lead. By late fall Mom was pregnant so she and Dan got married. Because Loyd had denied her those two shots to treat Rh when I was born, she needed regular testing and extensive medical care if this baby was going to make it. Her doctor visits and hospital stays grew more frequent and lasted longer the bigger her belly got. When my sister, Missy, finally came, everyone acted like she was some big miracle. I was jealous. Missy had to be in the hospital for ages and Mom stayed with her. Also, she was beautiful, with dark brown hair and olive skin. I worried everyone would forget me now that we had a pretty little miracle to adore. Somehow, I still fell under her spell.

On his days off, Dan went out for coffee, alternating between the café in Newberry's department store and a breakfast place called The Copper Kitchen. He'd sit alone reading the classified ads and smoking. Dan rarely ordered more than coffee. He enjoyed chatting with waitresses and tipped generously, pulling a folded wad of cash from his breast pocket. Sometimes, he'd take me along for hot chocolate and pancakes. I didn't look at the menu—he just ordered me pancakes. I knew this was a privilege and felt grateful, but couldn't exactly enjoy it. Dan was nice but I missed my daddy.

《 《 《

About the same time Jesse and I walked into that haunted house, Loyd walked into an AA meeting. He started bible study again and meetings at the Kingdom Hall, too. He sent us letters. When we first left they were frantic, his handwriting messy and inconsistent, letters arriving every couple of days. Now they slowed down, were neatly written, and signed off with *God bless you.* They even got a little apologetic, though he never outright apologized. Reading them now, I can see he was working the twelve steps.

Making amends. The cliché poetry of AA would work its way into our language like a regional accent. It still carries nostalgic beauty for me.

He came to visit us in The Dalles. He'd drive up to spend a day or two, take us to the park or public pool. We'd get shakes at Arctic Circle, fries with gravy at Johnny's café, burgers at Big Jim's. He tried to be funny, like nothing could keep his spirit down. *Let's go to Kentucky Fried Chicken. I like the way them plastic benches rumble when I rip one, know what I mean, Jess?* But he never really did that. He wanted us to think he wasn't afraid of our new life, our new town. But I could tell he was.

Pretty soon, Loyd brought Linda along to meet us. They were in AA together. Loyd said Linda was a pilot and had two daughters of her own but they lived with their dad. I'm pretty sure Linda was never a pilot, that this was Loyd's way of saying she'd been in the Air Force. He tended to polish and simplify. Linda approached us with caution, which felt right. I wasn't happy my parents were both moving on, but from the moment I met Linda I felt like she was meant to be part of my story. Linda's presence made Mom feel comfortable letting Loyd take us back to Clallam Bay for a visit.

Loyd had moved out of the double-wide on the bluff. He and Linda lived together in a little rented house out by the slip, near the field where Jesse used to play T-ball. We walked on the beach, sometimes lighting a fire down there, or sticking bottle rockets or sparklers in the wet sand and lighting them off. He let us use his pocketknife to whittle our own roasting sticks before cooking our hot dogs. Being back felt a lot like before we left but also very different. Now Linda was with us. She made us meals and washed our clothes. Because I was a girl, Linda took the lead on my upkeep.

Linda taught me to French braid my hair and told me I should keep my knees together if I ever wore a dress. At first, I think she was trying to treat me like she would her own daughters. She'd brush my hair one hundred strokes per section and remind me to wash properly in the bath. It was nice having Linda's help. It was better than Loyd, who'd holler from outside the door as I bathed, *don't forget to wash your spider!* I didn't even know what he meant by spider and I wasn't about to ask. Linda wasn't afraid of girlhood like Loyd was and that made it easier. But she was a little shocked by my way of being a girl.

I admit I enjoyed grating against Linda's propriety. It bothered her that I liked the tugging sensation of pulling a scab just enough, lifting my skin to that point right before it tears. Before long she accepted, even embraced, the dirt under my nails, that I wanted to wear Jesse's old jeans, and that I liked to wipe my hands on my pants, squatting to rub my palms back and forth on the tops of my thighs with a friction so strong she could hear it in the next room. And her acceptance was reciprocated.

Looking at Linda, I wanted to imagine her with more flesh. Her bone structure suggested plumpness. She had a full moon face and wide, round eye sockets, like a pumpkin. But she was thin, and her roundness seemed offended by the lack of flesh to fill it out. The geology of her face suggested something absent. I could smell a history of milk and baby powder. Motherhood can leave a scent like cigarette smoke clings to a body. We always want to touch soft things. I was sure her daughters couldn't keep their hands off her in better days, when she was supple. I could see sweet, clean baby hands reaching up to her smile, smooth fat fingers touching her mouth when it was still full of white teeth.

My body was happy to be in Clallam Bay again. The air west of the Cascades is still easier for me to breathe. Maybe that's because I was born in the woods and acclimated to green and damp during my formative years. I'd not yet learned the difference between a cedar and a pine, a hemlock and a spruce. I knew them by smell. I could taste fir on the air just as I could taste the ice that made a rushing creek by bending down to take a drink. The Dalles almost never had the smells of the forest. Standing next to, or even in, the Columbia, I had no sense where all that water came from. Scrubby pines dotted the hills but they only seemed to give off their scent on the hottest days and even then it was off-kilter. A heavy scent, not fresh. Pine dragged down by the heat of the sun, the smells of sage and roadside scotch broom.

But I missed my mom something fierce. Soon, I'd return to dry oaks, tall golden grass, and watchful hills dressed in brown. I'd learn to love the home my mom chose, to welcome the sunshine smile of balsamroot and purple lupine standing to greet each summer. But I'd never stop feeling the loss of the forest.

Loyd left Clallam County and started migrating again. He'd lost the job with Crown Zellerbach soon after Mom left him. Once he sobered up, he started with a smaller outfit but he quit because the state of Oregon attached his wages for child support. After that, Loyd only ever worked for cash or trade. After they married, Linda's wages were attached to pay Loyd's child support, so they legally divorced.

〈 〈 〈

Everyone always said I was the spitting image of my dad, a little piece of Loyd that broke off and grew legs. It didn't take Mom long to realize she hadn't completely left Loyd because his little piece was in the car with her when she drove away. Without Loyd to keep me in check, I started to throw mighty fits and I had my father's brand of singular focus for unreasonable rage.

My bad behavior was unpredictable, even to me. Maybe I'd want a pack of Hubba Bubba at the grocery store and Mom said no, maybe Jesse was hogging the Atari when it was clearly my turn. Maybe there was tone in my brother's voice, or he shared a dismissive glance with the neighbor kid. Whatever the stimulus, I could throw a grade-A shit fit and I'm telling you, I saw black when I did.

I could feel the temperature change come over my body, starting at my toes and moving up in a wave of red. When it hit my head, there was no stopping the outburst. I had to express it physically, there was no other way. I could run—that was especially effective in public. Frustration and worry washed over Mom's face when I'd disappear in Safeway or, even better, a parking lot or near a busy road. Seeing the fear I put on her face could satisfy my anger.

With Jesse I hit and thrashed. This was most cathartic in the end because it came with immediate consequences. Hitting Jesse ended with getting my ass kicked. I could purge my fury without having to feel guilty afterward that I hurt Mom's feelings. Jesse just gave me physical pain in return and there was a balance in that.

When I was angry with Mom, I'd often bring Loyd into it, let him help me beat her down. I'm deeply ashamed to admit it, but I would pull my dad from the ether and use him like a weapon. I'd run to my bed, jump up, stretch my body across the width, and swing my legs up, butt against the wall. Then I'd bend my knees so I could stomp, stomp, stomp, against the wall while I screamed.

I want my daddy! I want my daddy! I want my daddeeeee!

Even as I did this, I had a sense Loyd would approve. The swelling of pride I imagined in his chest pushed me on. Loyd had little ways he'd suggest our mom was to blame for the end of our family and I hadn't yet learned to know better. To trust my own memory over his bullshit.

If I had a fit like this at home, Mom just let me wear myself out. Her indifferent patience was the perfect antidote to my irrational violence. I'm so grateful for her half of me and to be able to say that I never hit my mom. She'd sit at the kitchen table, reading, and wait there to hold me when I'd eventually drag my exhausted, tear-stained, sorry ass out to her, head hanging in apology.

If we were in public, it was a whole other ball game. She wasn't about to let me get lost, kidnapped by some pervert, or ruin an innocent bystander's life by running out in front of their car and getting myself hit. My mom subscribed to a certain social order that was unspoken but clearly understood. We could be total assholes at home but we had better hold our shit together in public or there would be hell to pay. She started carrying a wooden spoon in her purse.

I learned the purpose of the wooden spoon in Fred Meyer. I never saw it come out and I was given no warning. One moment I was building up to a rage, then Mom's hand moved to her purse, out, and back again so fast I don't think a witness standing a foot away would've noticed. A sharp sting flashed across the backs of my thighs, stopping the red wave of anger right there, before it could creep farther up my body. She gripped my upper arm and led me out to the car, left our shopping cart right there in the middle of the frozen food section. Jesse was pissed at me. We had to eat leftover spaghetti for dinner because our tater tots and fish sticks were still in the cart, defrosting in the middle of the grocery store aisle. And that was my fault.

After that, going to the store with Mom was a privilege. If we were in public and she got even the slightest whiff of a fit coming on, her hand would move toward her purse. I'd see that wooden spoon with my X-ray vision, floating at the bottom of the bag with her pack of gum and car keys, and I'd rein myself right in. She carried it for quite some time but never had to use it again.

(((

We spent Christmas with Loyd and Linda in a rental house in Randle. Even though he was studying with the Witnesses again, Loyd did the whole Santa thing. I think he just really wanted us to have fun. He brought us outside on Christmas morning to see reindeer tracks in the snow. He pointed, squinting, at the roof where he swore he could just see the tracks continue all the way to the chimney. We had a tree and presents. Linda gave me a pair of red corduroy pants and I pretended I didn't like them much. But they were soft and I wore them until the knees had holes.

I screwed up Christmas dinner. We were all eating and I held my water cup in what I thought was a fancy posture. With my pinky sticking it out, I brought it to my lips, took a dainty sip and tried to talk like Miss Piggy.

Mmmm, this wine is delicious.

Loyd and Linda stopped eating. He reached out, grabbed my wrist, and pulled the cup away from my mouth. My water spilled a little. I always seemed to find a way to step in shit with Loyd but I wasn't sure what I'd done wrong. Even Jesse looked confused. We hadn't yet been to an AA meeting and didn't understand the puritan culture of Loyd's brand of sobriety. He looked like he was inching toward anger but Linda put her fork down and placed her palm on his shoulder. She spoke to me.

We do not pretend to drink alcohol in this house. OK, little missy?

Now I was super confused. I didn't see what the big deal was about pretending to drink wine. I wasn't even sure wine was alcohol because I didn't know anybody that ever drank wine. I'd never heard the term *little missy* before, I only knew it was my sister's name. I was offended that Linda would confuse me with my little sister. I set my cup down and spit out a snotty apology. But I wasn't sorry. I typed up a mental report and put the whole episode in my *reasons to hate Linda* file.

❨ ❨ ❨

In Morton we lived in a yellow cottage on a few acres. An old barn leaned toward the huge tree where a tire swung on a thick rope that burned the insides of my legs more times than I can count. And there were two ponies. I think Loyd was caretaking and the ponies came with the place, but he made it sound like he got them just for us. He let us name them but that doesn't mean they didn't already have other names. My pony was dirty white and I called her Princess. Jesse's was brown and he named her Brown Sugar, Sugar for short. Sugar was sweet and mellow so anyone could ride her. Princess was stubborn and testy. I guess they matched us personality-wise.

Mom and Dan were getting a divorce so Jesse and I went to school in Morton awhile. Morton Primary had a glass display case built into the wall near the office that always held some intriguing diorama, riddle, or contest. I won once. You had to guess the number of jellybeans in a fishbowl. I deserved it, too, because instead of just guessing I stood in front of the glass one afternoon and counted all the jellybeans I could see. Then I multiplied them, following a formula I made up to determine how many layers were in the bowl. I had a full page, front to back, of senseless calculations. I wasn't very good at math so I'm pretty sure that win was mostly luck. I don't recall what I got for winning, only that Jesse was annoyed.

He'd made a guess, too, and it was a violation of our sibling code that I won. I was his little sister. He was older and a boy. It was just like fishing. If I ever caught the first fish, everyone was quiet about it. If I caught a fish after Jesse, Loyd would celebrate and cheer and make a big deal, but there was some mysterious shame if Jesse didn't catch the first fish. I don't think either of us understood why.

Loyd had a big garden in Morton and we had regular chores. When I look at my middle-aged brother today, I can still see the towheaded boy who bossed me around that garden as we pulled weeds. He threw dirt clods when my back was turned, dared me to hold spiders or let pincher bugs hang from my finger. One time, he said he'd pay me a dollar to do all his chores. I pulled weeds and thought of all the ways I might spend that dollar, what combination of ten-cent candy boxes I'd buy and not share with him. Lemonheads, Red Hots, Boston Baked Beans. Or maybe I'd blow half of it on a pack of grape Hubba Bubba—just thinking of its smell made saliva well up in the back of my throat. Jesse would beg me for a piece and I liked to think I wouldn't give it to him. But we all knew I would. When I finished all the chores and asked for my dollar, Jesse pulled a single strand of silk from an ear of corn and handed it to me.

Here you go. One doll-hair. I got worked up, like he expected. I pushed and kicked at the injustice and before long he had me on my back in the dirt. He held me down and suspended a string of spit over my face.

If you don't calm down, I WILL spit on you. Nobody could push me into a frantic, wild fit like my brother. I told on him but Loyd thought Jesse's doll-hair joke was hilarious.

Good one, son!

We went to a lot of meetings in Morton. Loyd and Linda were trying to stay sober so that meant AA and church. Except instead of calling it *church*, Jehovah's Witnesses say *meeting*. So AA and religious services at the Kingdom Hall sort of ran together for me. Both had adults looking for salvation and adults who liked to be saviors. Both were held in fairly plain rooms with uncomfortable chairs, and boring prayers and poems. *God, grant me the serenity, If you love something, set it free, But for the grace of God.* I preferred the printed literature at the Kingdom Hall because at least the *Watchtower* and *Awake!* were colorful and sometimes had animals in them. But AA had coffee and an occasional cookie tray. I'd entertain Jesse by opening up little packets of powdered creamer and dumping them straight on my tongue.

One day, we were walking into the Kingdom Hall for a meeting and I noticed a dog tied up outside the doors. She was black and white and had clear blue eyes. I knelt down to pet her, both hands stretched forward on either side of her neck. Grit from the sidewalk pressed against my clean tights, pushing geological shapes into my knees and leaving smudges I knew would get me in some trouble. I was scratching her when a grown-up bent down close to me. He was a stranger with coffee breath. He smelled like cigarettes and Old Spice.

Hey now pretty girl, you don't want to get too close to that dog, she might not be gentle. I looked straight into her water-blue eyes and she smiled at my attention. Her warm breath washed over my face, a magic spell I wished could make me invisible. The man put his hand on my shoulder. I hoped ignoring him would make him go away but he kept talking to me.

He told me that you should never look into the eyes of a dog, or any other animal, because if you saw their soul they'd get angry and attack you, even if they seemed nice a minute before. He said that dog was likely to tear my face off if I got even a peek at her soul. I didn't let go or answer the man. I wanted him to know I'd rather take my chances with the dog than him. So I pretended he hadn't even said anything. I spoke only to the dog and only on our private channel, a frequency he couldn't hear. *Don't worry*, I told her, *I know you won't rip my face off.* Just to prove it, I leaned in and kissed her right on the nose. I let her lick my whole face. Then I got up, without a word or even a look for the man, and walked inside to join Loyd and Linda at another boring meeting.

Loyd had a classic truck back then. It was a black and silver 1950s GMC and I have no idea how he got his hands on it. He called it Sylvester because it was the colors of the cartoon cat always trying to catch Tweety bird. He had a lemon-scented Sylvester cat air freshener hanging from the rearview mirror and the black bench seat was covered with a multicolor woven seat cover because Loyd didn't like the way his cheeks stuck to it in summer.

One day, Loyd and I were cruising along in Sylvester and we passed a hitchhiker. Loyd drove on a bit, but then thought better of it and turned around. He pulled over just in front of the hitchhiker.

Where ya headed, buddy?

Tryin' to get to Yakima. Thought I had a ride but they ditched me in Mossyrock so I been patchin' it together since. Loyd said we could drop him in Randle. I got a bad feeling. He was bigger than Loyd and also very wide, with a belly bigger than Santa's spilling over the waistline of his stinky jeans. Loyd told me to scoot over and the man opened the door and climbed in, a serious effort.

As he hefted himself in, he exhaled a slow wave of nasty air toward me. He lifted a green army surplus style duffle and a bag from the market in Morton. I hoped his breathing might slow and quiet but it never did. Like lava crawling down a mountain, his breath soon coated everything in range with the stink of a man who's spent years killing his own liver. It was a hot day and the man smelled like dirty armpits and sour booze. He had a few days' worth of patchy stubble and long hairs coming out of his nose. Loyd was chatting with him and I knew he wanted me to be friendly, but I felt squeamish. This was a regular way I disappointed Loyd, my inability to charm his buddies. When I was comfortable with adults, I could really ham it up and let loose in a way Loyd found hilarious. Because he was constantly cycling through communities, I rarely got that comfortable with his friends.

As we pulled onto the road and took a wide corner, the hitchhiker slid into me. I felt like he'd done it on purpose. The sticky flesh of his arm pushed against mine and I imagined a germy sweat transfer, like he might infect me with something. I tried to hold my breath and sit still, but I just couldn't take it. I scooted as far away as I could, crunched up against my dad. As I moved away from him, the hitchhiker's damp skin peeled off mine like when you pull a Band-Aid away from its wrapper.

I was watching straight out the windshield when the hitchhiker cleared his throat, reached into the paper grocery sack, and offered Loyd a beer.

Cold one, buddy?

Now this guy was in for a talking-to. I waited for Loyd to let loose his special blend of AA/Watchtower Society preaching. I was ready to hear the Good News and all about letting go to a Higher Power. Maybe I'd even make Loyd proud and pipe in with *just take it one day at a time* or *let God and let go.* For this situation *one drink is too many and a thousand is never enough* seemed to fit. But Loyd waited. He consulted first the angel on his left shoulder, then the devil on his right, and accepted the beer. It was a can of Rainier, still cold from the store.

Whenever I saw the Rainier Beer commercial, I thought of Loyd. Motorcycle climbing up a tree-lined country road under the gaze of Mt. Rainier, engine whining out the name—RaaaiiiiniiieeeerrrrBeeeer—as it shifted. Loyd often lived on or around Mt. Rainier and I'd always known him to drink beer. Also the shifting motorcycle engine sounded like a chainsaw at work. The sound of a chainsaw chewing through wood was my daddy's song.

The hitchhiker opened up the beer. I swear I could see a look like prayer on Loyd's face with the crack of that beer tab. The sound of pressure releasing out of that can felt like it was coming straight from Loyd. The hitchhiker's arm crossed in front of my face, his armpit smell rising to sting my eyeballs, as he handed it over. Loyd took a long swig and I could see it was like coming home after forty years in the desert. Loyd pushed the sweating can into his crotch and sighed a relaxed exhale. Before long the meetings slowed, then stopped. Then it was time to go back to Mom.

(((

Leaving Dan left Mom flat broke. We had to move to the west side of The Dalles and she went to work full-time. Lots of kids on the west side lived in trailer parks or apartment buildings but we were able to rent a small house because Aunt Ruth's boyfriend owned it and gave Mom cheap rent as long as he could occasionally stay there. He sometimes had construction jobs that kept him in town for a couple of weeks at a time. Mom hated when he stayed with us. We all did. He expected us to behave and would punish us if he saw fit. The house was a single level, the slab of concrete foundation covered in thin linoleum for the interior floor. There were a few others like it in the neighborhood, built back when the aluminum plant was booming and they needed to build houses fast. Most families with aluminum jobs could eventually afford to move to the east side so their kids could go to school in district twelve. Now the street was almost all single moms.

It was a new era of freedom for us kids. Mom worked in housekeeping at the hospital during the week and had her weekend job at JCPenney, so we were in charge of ourselves a lot. We ran around the neighborhood, loitered at Dehart's market, skimmed the top of the dumpster behind the Sixth Street gas station. We found our way down to Chenowith Creek and could almost pretend we were in the woods again.

But it was hard, too. Jesse and I fought all the time. I'd often call Mom at work, crying or even bleeding. We mostly fought over who had to let Missy follow them around all day, who needed to put the toaster away or sweep the kitchen. Nonsense. In the morning on our way to school, we'd walk Missy to the babysitter. She lived in a trailer park everyone called *felony flats*. One day we had early release and I came to pick Missy up just in time to see the babysitter's boyfriend backhand her and send her little body flying across the room. I didn't speak, not sure I could've. Keeping my eyes on Missy I barged in, scooped her up, and left. Mom, Jesse, and I took turns calling in sick until we could line up a new sitter.

There was a bowling alley right down the block on Chenowith Loop Road and Mom joined the league. She was really good. She always looked forward to league night. We'd walk over and pester her for quarters to play the arcade games. Mostly Space Invaders or pinball because we had Pac-Man at home. About this time something bad went down between Loyd and Linda so they split up. Dad started calling Mom all the time, telling her he loved her and would take care of her and all three of us kids if she'd come back. She got drawn in, the idea of escaping our oppressive landlord, not having to work so much and leave her kids all the time. Before long, Mom told us we were going to be a family again.

She gave two weeks notice at the hospital and started packing up our stuff. She was planning to leave right after her bowling team finished the season. They kept winning. With each delay, Loyd grew more impatient. Mom's team won the final tournament, which meant they got a free trip to compete in Reno. She was so excited. She'd never been on a vacation.

She called Loyd with the news and he told her that no wife of his was going to Reno with a bunch of other men, staying in hotels, drinking, and who knows what else. The morning after that phone call, Mom went to the hospital and asked for her job back. She got it, but no time off so she couldn't go to Reno. It wasn't long before Loyd and Linda were back together.

I had this little exercise I invented. Kind of like a fire drill at school. I liked how fire and earthquake drills gave me power over my fate. I wasn't afraid of natural disasters. Though I vaguely remembered the eruption of Mount St. Helens and the faint layer of ash that settled over my world, it was too far away to be scary for me. But I knew a different sort of catastrophe, the kind grown-ups created. I liked the idea that, with careful planning and practice, I could keep myself safe.

Missy and I had this cheap, beat-up chest in our room. It held our toys. Calling it a toy box is generous to both the box and its contents. But there aren't always the right words—I find that true when I want to describe the tossed-off things that are gathered up by the poor. We had lots of stuff like that and I'm still prone to rescuing the useful and discarded.

I'd empty the chest and stash toys around our room. Five Barbie dolls with ratty hair, one with a slightly melted face. A stuffed Grover from Sesame Street, his blue fur worn away where I used to stroke around his glass eyes. Missy's plastic yellow telephone with eyes that moved up and down as she pulled it along on its short red string. Hiding the toys took awhile because some had bells or other noisy parts. I needed to be quiet and deliberate with my movements. Nobody could know the chest was empty. That would ruin it. Once it was empty, I'd roll up my pale blue waffle knit blanket and place it in the chest alone.

When it was time to practice, I'd open the chest and unroll the blanket outward, perpendicular to the chest so together they formed a T. I'd lie down at the far end of the blanket, my body parallel to the chest, and roll toward it, wrapping my whole body in the blanket as I went. When I bumped against the chest, I'd arch my back, stick up my butt in the air like an inchworm, and push it over the rim of the chest. My cocooned body fell in with a soft thump. It was always my struggle, to silence that thump. I'd free my right hand to reach up and close the lid, real slow.

Panic rushed me right here. I hated small spaces. I had to learn to ride out that wave of alarm and not let it cause jerky, loud movements. Then, I had to work my free arm back inside the blanket to make sure every part of me was covered. Not a hair sticking out. If someone were to open the chest, they shouldn't be able to tell I was inside. They'd just see a folded-up blanket.

I was claustrophobic. Jesse was forever holding me down with a pillow or trapping me inside a sleeping bag. This entire safety drill was designed not only as a perfect hiding place in case of danger, but also to cure my fear of tight spaces. In case I ever needed to hide. It's an important skill, to be able to disappear.

close call

LOYD AND LINDA RENTED a neat, white farmhouse on the edge of Yakima. It sat on a large lot of bright lawn, with a scraggly old pine to the west, overgrown yew and holly shrubs, and a small wooden shed with white paint peeling off in flakes like snow. That shed was my favorite thing about the place in Yakima. It reminded me of the witch's candy cottage in "Hansel and Gretel." The lawn surrounding the little house sparkled green against the patchy browns of Yakima in summer. Loyd watered the place from a concrete-lined irrigation ditch that cut through the middle of the property. A wood-plank bridge ran over the ditch to Loyd's garden on the other side. They could afford the rent because the place sat right in the center of a web of roads connecting to Highway 82. We could constantly smell and hear engines but still, it was charming.

Mom drove us up that summer and Loyd thanked her by filling her trunk with carrots, lettuce, green beans, cukes, and a couple of early tomatoes. Before we arrived Loyd got us a dog. She was a little black mutt he'd picked up at the pound. I think Loyd wanted Mom to see how happy we were at the surprise.

I marched right into that dog pound, he said, and told them to bring me the next mutt headed to the gas chamber! It sounded like something Loyd would do. The dog they brought him had stubby legs that couldn't ever give her the speed she wanted. He called her CC, for Close Call, and he loved telling everyone how she got her name, how he was her savior.

I wanted to resist CC because I sensed my dad trying to win some pissing match with Mom. Not for our love, exactly. It was more like he still felt the need to demonstrate what she lost when she'd walked away. I wanted to be neutral. Going all gaga over this dog felt like a betrayal of my Mom. She was always doing all the work while Loyd had all the fun.

And I knew right off I'd regret loving that dog. She was the sort of thing that never stays. But I couldn't help myself. CC was amazing. She approached me with patience, as if she understood my reluctance. Like she knew we were both caught up in a current we had no control over. Our first encounter was simple. She walked up slowly and put her nose to my hand. Her warm breath was an invitation to intimacy that no other creature had ever extended me.

CC had the magic effect of bringing Jesse and me together. She was the thing we agreed on. Her sweetness was untouchable, her loyalty miraculous. We didn't compete for her affection. CC loved us both so we both must be worth loving. We played with her together and didn't fight about it.

She'd follow us to the shed, our pretend drive-thru restaurant. The shed had a rectangular window that slid open sideways, like at McDonald's, and it was just our height. A little shelf was nailed to the wall inside, right under the window. One of us would stand there, working, while the other approached from outside to order food. CC usually went through the drive-thru with the customer, but sometimes she'd stretch out in a spot of sun in the corner of the shed, supervising. We filled orders by making food from anything we could find. Mud pies decorated with dusty bluish juniper berries; salads of crabgrass, dandelions, and clover; burger patties made by beating mud and pine needles between our hands.

We'd call out to CC from hiding places and giggle as she whined, worried, trying to find us. We might be under a blanket or in a tree, or calling from two different places at once. Jesse would pretend to throw a stick and yell, *go fetch, girl!* But hold the stick tight. She'd run after it anyway.

We never got tired of her attention and I don't think we resented any CC-related chores.

Loyd loved her, too. He taught her a few basic tricks and let her up on the couch with him to watch TV and eat popcorn. He called her his *football buddy*, because she watched the Seahawks with him. He was pleased that she learned fast never to go into his garden. No need for a fence to keep her out.

Jesse and I tried to coax CC into the garden when Loyd wasn't around, but she refused to cross the plank bridge over the irrigation ditch. She followed us everywhere but as soon as we stepped on the bridge, she'd sit in the grass, waiting. We got it in our heads she was afraid of the bridge or water running below. So Jesse picked her up and carried her into the garden. The second he set her down she bolted back across the bridge and sat in the grass.

The house had a little screened-in back porch. Loyd set it up with a string of blue Christmas lights, a wicker couch he'd found next to a dumpster, a couple of odd chairs, and his boom box. He'd sit out there evenings drinking, smoking, and listening to his *tunes*. He loved Charlie Daniels, Willie Nelson, and Hank Williams, but also James Brown, Janis Joplin, and Jimi Hendrix. You just never knew with Loyd. That summer he was having a Frankie Goes to Hollywood phase. He liked listening to "Relax" while basking in blue light. We'd hear "Relax" end, the click and whir of Loyd rewinding the tape, "Relax" start again.

That was the first time I noticed his homemade cigarettes, *funny smokes*, he called them. I guess that was his way of not lying about his marijuana use. When I was grown and looking at old photos, I'd notice a pot plant or two, growing in old buckets on the edge of pretty much every garden he ever kept.

Loyd was logging that summer, so he got up before dawn and left long before we woke. *Gotta stay ahead of the heat, kids.* They'd start around four in the morning, quit by one. Sometimes, he'd choose one of us to wake up with him for coffee before work. I never found a pattern to predict what days he'd do this or which kid he'd pick. It was a silent, dreamlike privilege.

Dad's voice would pull me from sleep, about as soft as I'd ever heard it, his hands rocking my shoulders. I'd follow him down the short, narrow stairs to the kitchen. He'd pour coffee in two milky green mugs, as if we were equals. He put sugar in both but encouraged me to add more if I wanted, pushing the sugar bowl my way. I always added more and he never shamed me for it. We didn't talk much, just sat together drinking our coffee while Loyd smoked a couple cigarettes in the cool dark. Then he'd gather his lunch pail and thermos. Send me back to bed and leave for work, the wood screen door clattering gently behind him.

I'd fall asleep trying to hold on to every detail, thinking how I'd mention it to Jesse, like it was no big deal. Usually, I didn't tell him at all. I kept it for myself. I'm certain he sometimes did the same.

Linda would wake us around 7:30, if we weren't up yet, serve us cereal or oatmeal, and send us out to do our chores. We were supposed to stay in the garden and work on the list Loyd left until lunch. Chores never took us that long but I think Linda just needed us out of her hair.

Sometimes I imagine Linda standing at the kitchen sink in Yakima, looking out at us pulling weeds in the garden. What did she feel? What thoughts went through her head as she watched us, perpetually dirty and wearing T-shirts too tight, pants too short? Proud to collect scars, always in need of haircuts, independent in ways that testified to the lack of adult supervision in our daily lives.

I bet she stood there thinking of her own two daughters. Their wheat-blond hair, so light and fine their eyebrows disappeared in summer, and their blue eyes. They were the cleanest kids I'd ever met. Pristine and polite, their clothing coordinated and they never had holes in their socks. Even their pajamas were matching sets. I only met them once or twice and I couldn't tell if Linda saw them sometimes without us, or if she just didn't see them much. Mom sent Loyd school pictures every year. The pictures Linda had of her girls hardly ever changed and I took that to mean their dad didn't bother much to keep in contact.

Those girls are what Linda lost. I never learned the details of how or why. Linda was a different sort of addict than Loyd. She was the tortoise to his hare. He was binge, explode, purge. All speed and wiry energy. Linda was slow and steady wins the race. She walked through space like the air around her was thick. Her movements were usually slow and careful.

Linda had been raised in a nice home by parents who seemed fancy to me. I'd only met them briefly but I imagined her dad read books and her mom used words like *poise*. Linda had been on trips that required airplanes. She'd married a man with a steady job and owned a home. Her kids had college savings and excused themselves to go to the bathroom if they needed to pass gas.

Loyd had never fallen from grace because he'd never known it. He came from backwoods trash and was happy that way. He'd ask anyone, anywhere, to pull his finger. But Linda seemed different. I remember visiting her parents in Ellensburg. Their house reminded me of a commercial for Glade air freshener, with white curtains and a wide porch. I thought she must really love Loyd to leave that sort of life behind. Looking back, I think clean living made Linda feel ugly. I think she was afraid everything she touched was made dirty by her hands. She was constantly washing her hands. That's why Linda, of all the players in Loyd's travelling shit-show, scares me the most.

Linda's life with Loyd wasn't a natural extension of what she'd always known. Her life was loss, constant penance for her addictions. She'd slept in clean beds under duvets that smelled like fabric softener. Now she slept under a rough green army surplus blanket and moved from rental to trailer to shack, from one small mill town to another. Now she rarely saw her daughters and when she did, she felt undeserving. Now her teeth were rotting out. Now she worked at a dive café, adding water, then more mix, then more water, carefully trying to balance out the pancake batter every morning.

And now, I imagine she stands at that kitchen window in Yakima and looks out at Jesse and me crouching in the garden, our bare knees sunk directly into soft dirt. We were the kind of children she wasn't afraid to touch. I would reach both palms down and thrust them forward in the soil, letting it flow through my fingers, over my hands, all the way up to my elbows, and my little body would sing with the earthly pleasure of it. How could she resist comparing me to her own lovely daughters, angelic in their inaccessibility? In my strange fantasy, she thinks of them, practicing piano or flute in the light-filled house she left behind. Being dropped off by their father at ballet class or softball practice. And, I imagine, she felt sure of her choice. Keeping her distance preserved them.

We had an unspoken arrangement with Linda that summer in Yakima. As long as we stayed out in the garden until lunch, she didn't care what we were doing. Our chores were done in the first hour and we spent the rest of the morning playing secret games in the garden. Secret because we weren't allowed to play in Loyd's garden.

The forbidden nature of our garden games made them more fun. We loved coming up with ways to play during chore time. We snuck out small toys—green army men or Matchbox cars—in our pockets. Jesse had the entire set of cars from the *Dukes of Hazzard* and we'd build roads to act out episodes we'd seen. We raced boats made of leaves in the current of the irrigation ditch. The endless supply of dirt and water kept us busy making mud pies and sculptures. We thought it was funny to sculpt anything offensive and before long we had an ongoing competition to see who could make the most realistic pile of mud dog poo.

No matter what games we played, we were careful to destroy all evidence before going in to lunch. We might spend all morning excavating our version of Hazzard County in the dirt so we could make Rosco's police car crash into a pile of twigs stacked up like lumber as he chased Bo and Luke Duke. No matter how carefully we crafted our play world, we made sure no trace was left. Every game of tic-tac-toe in the dirt was wiped away, every mud sculpture crumbled up and spread about like it never existed.

Loyd inspected his garden after work, still in his thick pants and suspenders, covered in sweat and sawdust. First, he'd go in the house and grab cold beers and the tin saltshaker. He kept a folding chair in the garden. He'd set it up, sit down, cross right leg over left, and open his first beer. After a bit he'd stand, pick up the chair, and move to another spot. In each spot he'd sample his produce, sprinkled with salt, drink beer, and check our work.

It made me anxious. I'd wonder if we'd thinned the carrot seedlings well, or missed any of the fat green caterpillars we were supposed to pick off the undersides of the tomato leaves. Was the bean patch carefully weeded and had we tied up all the stray vines? I might feel shame in this moment, for the games we played. I'd worry they kept us from doing a good job.

But we were actually pretty good at our chores. We were used to being independent. At home with Mom, we got ourselves up and off to school every day. We woke Missy, made sure she was dressed and fed, and walked her to her babysitter on our way. Sure, we liked to screw around and we had filthy mouths with our friends. We hit and scratched each other when we fought, but we were pretty responsible and capable. Loyd was usually pleased with our work.

He'd sometimes call us out to the garden while he was out there and we'd walk out slowly, afraid we'd done something wrong. He almost always wanted to share something wonderful. A bird's nest or first bloom. *Here, try this cuke.* He held his pocketknife in his right hand, his thumb along the back of the blade, and ran it through the cucumber in one smooth cut, then held it to my mouth so I could eat the slice right off the blade. Knife in his right hand, cucumber in his left, saltshaker between his knees and beer beside his left ankle.

Jesse and I were running in the grass one afternoon when Loyd came home from work. We were playing tag with CC. Whoever she touched was it so we'd run from her and try to get her to touch the other person. We were barefoot, our skinny, tanned bodies poking out of too-small shorts and tank tops. Loyd stopped and gave us each a kiss on our sweaty heads on his way out to the garden. He'd been out there about forty-five minutes when he called for her.

CC!

She froze. The hair on her back stood up and her tail sank. Like us, she knew when to fear Loyd's voice. I wondered if she saw what I saw when that voice growled out of him. For the first time, I was curious how she'd learned never to go in the garden. What lessons had the wolf taught her? I loved her so very much in that moment.

Come here, CC! I knew Loyd was mad when he pronounced the 'h' in *here*. CC tried to obey. She went toward him but he was in the garden so she stopped and sat in the grass instead of crossing the bridge. My throat was nearly closed but I squawked out.

What's the matter, Daddy? I tried to sound as small as possible.

That damn dog's been in my garden! I knew this wasn't true.

No, Daddy, she never goes in the garden, I said.

We've been out here with her all day, Jesse added.

Then why is there dog shit in my garden, huh? He paused, then called her again.

Come HERE, CC! This time he pointed his finger down at the ground beside his feet. This gesture would normally bring her to him without words.

Jesse and I shared a look of sad shame. We knew the answer to his question. There was dog shit in Loyd's garden because one of us had sculpted it from mud. There was dog shit in Loyd's garden because we had missed it during our careful clearing up. There was dog shit in Loyd's garden and now someone had to pay.

And the three of us, boy, girl, and dog, knew who it would be. My brother and I settled the matter with sibling telepathy. We knelt beside CC facing the bridge, each with a hand on her, and I have never felt more ashamed of myself. Whatever bravery and self-sacrifice had pulsed through me moments before was swallowed up by pure, terrified self-preservation. We were cowards. We were selfish kids who played when we should have been working and now our sweet CC was gonna take it for us.

Each time we started a visit with Loyd, we stepped into the joy, adventure, and danger of a fairy tale. Loyd was creative and fun but this transformation was part of his nature. There was a release that came with it. We knew ways to disappear, stay hidden while the wolf prowled. Hitting put the wolf to sleep. If we were lucky, he'd get in a fight with another drunk. Sometimes he hit Linda. We understood our part in the story. It was our job not to notice, to pretend we didn't hear or see anything. But we'd never had a CC before, an innocent to keep safe. We no longer walked through the fairy tale alone. We had a true companion. And like many heroes, we didn't deserve our brave sidekick.

CC sat in the grass and looked across the bridge at Loyd. He called again but she stayed. He crossed the bridge, pushing a wave of malice ahead of him like thick, hot air we could all feel. She darted away and sat again, farther off. Loyd came at her, she darted again. This could've been a funny story, had Loyd been a gentler man. We could've laughed each year at the Thanksgiving table as he scratched the geriatric dog behind her ears and retold the comedy of his pursuit and her agility, eluding him each time.

But Loyd was not that kind of man and, after missing her a few times all he could see was black. The wolf was among us. Before I could even consider confession, his anger flared into such a brilliant white-hot flame that there was no way I could put myself in his path. Our entire lives had taught us not to. Our bodies had memories we couldn't call up but they animated us anyway. I moved out of his periphery but didn't run and hide like I normally would. I couldn't leave CC completely.

I watched in slow motion. Rushing white noise filled my head. Before he grabbed the shovel, I already knew he would. I'd seen his eyes dart to it, leaning against the quaint white shed where we'd spent so many sunny afternoons. I wonder if CC was drawn to the shed because it felt safe to her, if this was another way I was responsible. Loyd reached for the shovel as he ran by, trying to cut her off when she circled the shed. My confession tried to belch out but my voice stuck, a solid thing in my throat. I wanted to be brave. I wanted to tell the truth. But I was only weak and ashamed. He pursued her, shovel raised above his head.

I heard CC yelp when Loyd caught up to her. Heard the shovel make contact. I ran into the house after that first yelp. I was useless now, my witness a betrayal. I've often wondered if Loyd meant to kill her, or if it was an accident of his anger.

He came in awhile later. I was lying on my little bed, facing the wall. He tried to tell me a version of the truth. He said CC jumped out into the highway as she ran from him, that he thought she ran off but he was awful worried. So much traffic. I knew it was a lie. His entire body betrayed him. I could feel remorse coming off him like I can feel rays from the sun. He said he was sorry but I kept my back to him out of fear or anger or both.

We never saw CC again. I tried to believe she'd run away to a new family. I wished for a calmer dad, more deserving children. I let her disappear from memory. It was just easier that way. I know CC never ran away. I know Loyd beat her to death with that shovel. Jesse told me. He didn't stay until the very end but longer than I did. Long enough to see she wouldn't get up when it was over.

Soon after, Jesse noticed the freshly upturned oval of earth in the far corner of the yard, near the huge pine tree. We gravitated to that area, played in the shade of the pine. I can picture Loyd, laying CC to rest, bent over. Hoping physical labor would purge his guilt. We were adults when Jesse confirmed that was CC's grave, and a playful smile forced itself across his lips. Even now, our bodies participate in this involuntary defense, colluding in Loyd's stories, trying to make humor of tragedy.

《 《 《

When it was about time to go back home to Mom, Loyd took us to Kmart and told us we could each pick one thing that cost $100 or less. Even though I was getting old enough to know this wasn't right, that he didn't help Mom with money but could buy us unnecessary toys, I wasn't going to pass up the opportunity. Going to Kmart and spending $100 was the sort of thing we saw in movies. This was Little Orphan Annie and Daddy Warbucks territory. We were helpless to resist such luxury.

When you imagine a poor kid, you might picture a scrappy but responsible and selfless character like Little Orphan Annie. That's not what I was like. Most of the time I was a selfish little jerk. My siblings and I would fight like dogs over small things, each desperate to get the largest piece of whatever good thing came our way.

As a treat, Mom sometimes bought us a box of sweet cereal, like the generic versions of Cap'n Crunch or Froot Loops that came in a bag instead of a box. Like dog food. Getting candy cereal was like a holiday. We'd get up early and eat it until we were sick, just to hog as much as possible before our siblings could. Mom made a rule that we could each only have one bowl a day. Jesse used a mixing bowl, pouring in nearly the entire bag at once.

I had a secret habit of binging on Children's Tylenol because I thought it tasted like candy. As a hospital employee, Mom got a discount if she bought them in big boxes, like at the doctor's office. Each dose in a tiny packet, foil inside, white paper outside. Mom noticed they were disappearing but none of us confessed. She sat us down for a lecture on the danger of taking too much medicine and hid the box. I tried hard to resist. But they were so delicious I found myself sneaking around until I found them in her closet. I think the foil packets were meant to be childproof but I used her fingernail clippers to get them open.

I decided five at a time was probably not going to kill me. It felt like a conservative number. As soon as the first one hit my tongue, I was thinking about the next. I could only enjoy the chalky tang for a brief second before I was anxious about it being gone. Sometimes, I couldn't help myself and ate six or seven, then worried myself sick thinking I might die from it. When I was done I'd go the kitchen trash can, lift out some garbage, and stash the Tylenol packets underneath. I'm sure my siblings had similar secrets. We had appetites. We wanted stuff.

When Loyd took us to Kmart I was faced with a crisis of identity. It was the sort of occasion where your true colors are forced to shine. Jesse knew we should get bikes. We were in charge of getting ourselves to school and were always wishing we had bikes to ride in the morning. Mom couldn't afford new bikes so we'd scraped ours together by taking apart old bikes and parts we found at Hi-Dollar John's. Well, Jesse did anyway.

Grandpa Pothead owned a junkyard called Hi-Dollar John's. *Owned* is a stretch. He rented a bunch of land down by the railroad tracks at the east end of The Dalles and traded in junk there. He helped pay the bills by renting out beds in the abandoned trailers scattered around the property. He charged homeless men $1 a night for a bed, which might mean there'd be two or three guys in a trailer at once. No water, no sewer, no power. There were chickens scratching around the junkyard and it smelled like rancid oil and rust. Pothead let Jesse dig around for parts to cobble together bikes but they were pretty crappy. They were always losing pieces and in need of tweaking so we didn't rely on them to get us to school.

When we walked into Kmart Jesse assumed we were on the same page. He went straight for the bike section and I knew he was right. There they stood, lined up in a neat row. Every piece of them brand new and in working order. Every kind and color we could want, bright banana seats, BMX knock-offs. Jesse started test-driving and I felt sick to my stomach. He looked at me, eyebrows pulled together, and told me which bike I should try first. Maybe he thought I was overwhelmed by my options. It's true I had no idea how to pick a new bike, but that wasn't the holdup.

I wanted a Cabbage Patch Kid. I wanted to keep up with other girls at school and a bicycle wasn't going to help me do that. Every girl that mattered had at least one Cabbage Patch Kid. Some had several. Some had whole trunks of clothing and accessories. I only wanted one. One, with her carefully selected eye and hair color, her factory-prescribed name and, most intriguing, her official adoption papers. A Cabbage Patch Kid meant social acceptance for me and I was pretty sure this was my only chance to get one.

Damn Loyd and his loaded gifts. I knew this one would be painful for Mom. She understood how desperate I was to own a Cabbage Patch Kid. She just couldn't afford the expense. They didn't sell them at the small JCPenney where she worked on the weekends.

Mom's JCPenney job was how she bought us school clothes and shoes. She could use her employee discount and put things on layaway. She'd slowly purchased our microwave and VCR this way. We were lucky if the small JCPenney in The Dalles happened to carry something we really wanted for Christmas because she was likely to put it on layaway for us.

Mom knew a lady who lived in Foley Lakes, a trailer park where I never saw any lakes. The lady had a bright AstroTurf lawn. A six-inch-tall, plastic white picket fence lined her flowerbed, full of fabric tulips and daffodils that bloomed all year on green plastic stems. She made Cabbage Patch rep-

licas for less than half the price. Mom ordered one and traded some cleaning and errands for part of the payment.

When Mom asked me what hair and eye colors I'd choose, I thought
for sure I was getting a Cabbage Patch for Christmas. When I opened the
homemade version, I didn't hide my disappointment well. My mom had
more faith in me than I deserved. She thought I wanted a doll to play with,
to dress, to love. She probably thought I liked the novelty of picking the
hair and eye color. But I was less authentic than that. I wanted a trophy. I
wanted to be as good as the girls who had Cabbage Patch Dolls and, maybe
more important, I wanted to be better than those who didn't.

I named the knockoff Mary Lou, after the gymnast Mary Lou Retton,
who appeared in these little fitness segments between Saturday morning
cartoons. I'm not sure why—I wasn't into fitness or gymnastics. I actually
did play with Mary Lou a lot but I was private about it. I didn't want Mom
to think I was satisfied because I still wanted the real thing. Like I said
before, I was selfish. I knew Mom was hurt that I wasn't grateful for Mary
Lou. I also knew there was no way I could show up with that doll at school.

And now Loyd handed me the chance to get the real thing. Jesse had
picked out his new bike and was waiting for me. I was still on the first bike
he'd suggested I try. I rode in a slow, thoughtful circle around the long rack
of bikes, figuring out how to break the news to him. Mom was constantly
forcing him to escort me places and he did all the maintenance on our
junkyard bikes. If I didn't get a new bike, it would impact him.

I thought about asking Loyd to bring me back later, so I could have
more time to think. But that was too risky. Loyd's intentions changed with
his moods and we were here, now. This was my chance. I was standing
under the lights of Kmart and I swear I could hear the Cabbage Patch Kids
calling to me not three aisles away. I had to man up and face my brother.

C'mon already—pick one and let's go! He was ready to go out and ride
his new bike. I decided silence was the best option. I got off the cherry red
Huffy, parked it back in its rack, and walked away.

Where are you going? His lip was curled, his chest a little in front of his
body, aiming toward me. He was using ancient big brother sign language

to let me know I was out of line. As we grew, we'd stop using this language with one another. I started making my own decisions, instead of always deferring to him. I didn't respond, just kept walking.

Where are you going?

I stepped in front of a wall of adorable babies, harvested from the magical cabbage patch by Xavier Roberts just for me. Different-colored eyes beamed out at me from countless little vinyl heads. Variations of hair color, clothing, skin tone created the illusion of diversity among them. But really they were all the same faced, same bodied, same boxed. Still, I looked at them and knew there would be no bike.

Jesse figured out what I was thinking. He tried to correct my behavior.

What? No! No way, stupid!

I knew he was right. But I could just imagine what it would feel like to walk the halls of Chenowith Primary with that doll. How important it would be to keep from beaming, how hard I'd work to play it cool, because nothing reeks poor white trash like showing too much pride when you finally acquire a piece of the social currency of your betters. We stood before the wall of Cabbage Patch Kids and Loyd asked if I wanted one. I nodded.

Alrighty then, which one?

The answer was dictated by a rule among my peers. Your first Cabbage Patch should have the same hair and eye color as you. I needed one with yellow hair and green eyes. Loyd started helping me look. Brown hair. Blue eyes. Black Hair. Brown eyes. I'm not proud but I shit you not, I tasted bile in the back of my throat. It meant that much. In an act of fatherly heroism Loyd started moving the first layer of babies to check behind. Despite his better judgment, Jesse jumped in to help and together we tore that wall down.

We had a couple false positives, Jesse or Loyd bringing a doll over to me like an offering, just to have me reject it. Finally my brother, god among brothers, pulled a blonde-haired, green-eyed doll from among the masses and presented her to me with confidence. She was perfect. We walked away, triumphant.

I was a little disappointed with her name, Aloverta Roberta. I'd have preferred a Tiffany or a Nicole. But her name had been assigned at Baby-land General Hospital by people who knew better than me. I nicknamed her Allie.

I kept Allie in her box and that bothered Loyd. He couldn't under-stand why I didn't play with her. I wanted to keep her pristine. I did take her out a little each day. First I'd wash my hands, obviously. But I couldn't resist handling her. She smelled like fresh plastic and baby powder, her cheeks smooth and cool. I'd read and replace her adoption papers. Someday I'd fill them out and mail them in but not just yet. Unboxing and boxing the doll became a ritual performed with the precision and simplicity of a tea ceremony. Each piece of packaging was replaced, each plastic-coated wire re-twisted. Like a factory reset, she was untouched again each time.

Jesse was harsh with me for a few days and I knew I deserved it. As I sat alone performing my strange ritual, it was difficult to block out the joyful sounds of him riding his bike outside with the neighbor kids. Like every friend I ever made with Loyd, I'd never see these kids again. I'd forget their names. I used to squeeze in as much friend time as possible before leaving Loyd. Now I didn't see the point. All creatures, human or otherwise, that Loyd brought into our lives were temporary. The doll would stay with me.

Back at Mom's things were pretty much the same. Allie stayed in her box. In private I'd take her out, handle her, put her back in. On the first day of school I planned to carelessly sling her into my book bag, like she wasn't a big deal. I kept her up on my dresser. I walked into our room one day and noticed Allie was askew in her box. Her posture was wrong, her twisty ties on the ground at the foot of the dresser.

I lifted her down from her perch and drew a slow breath. Her face was written all over with permanent marker in Missy's distinct artistic style. I raged, I wept, I think I even hit my toddler sister, which is inexcusable. I mean, she was barely potty trained. Mom tried everything to soothe me and broker peace but I wouldn't have it. I know she felt terrible for me because she didn't even spank me when I committed Mom's most despised crime, yelling *I HATE YOU!* at Missy. Mom just walked away and let me wail in my bed.

After a while Mom came in with Allie in her hands. Her plastic face was miraculously clear. I jumped up to inspect closer. Mom told me she'd spent the last hour cleaning Allie's face with a Q-tip and nail polish remover. My exhausted mother, who rarely got a day off, probably just wanted to sit at the kitchen table with her feet up, drink coffee, smoke a couple of cigarettes, and read the damn romance novel she'd picked up at a yard sale. Instead, she'd spent all morning soothing my disappointment, then repairing this doll whose value to me evaporated the moment marker touched her face.

And now she held the doll toward me, handling it with care to show respect for this object that clearly meant so much to me. She tried to honor that, even if she couldn't understand. She waited for my response, probably a little cautious. After all, the black hole of want in my center was the reason she had to carry a wooden spoon in her purse. I looked at Allie.

There's still marker in her eye, I sniffled out.

Let me just say, I can see how the awful protagonist of this story maybe deserves her fate. But I really didn't know any better. Countless little cues, repeated every day of my life, taught me I might climb socially by owning stuff. I couldn't go to a friend's birthday party up on the mountain because I didn't have ski gear. Couldn't pay the fee or buy the shoes to be on the basketball team with my friends. Kids like me leaned on commercial crap all the time to make us feel part of the social conversation. My older cousin, a teen mom and my hero, lived in subsidized apartments and depended on food stamps but made damn sure her kids had every single Disney movie on VHS. And when she bought clothing for those kids, one shirt with Mickey Mouse on it was better than two without, everyone knew that.

Allie's left eye was wonky. The smallest swipe of black streamed out of the pupil and into the green iris. It might've been imperceptible if not for the simple symmetry of the eyes calling attention to any difference. This fraction of evidence was enough to reignite my despair.

I asked Mom if she could correct Allie's deformed eye. She explained that the eye looked to be painted on so nail polish remover would probably take off the eye along with the marker. I mustered a sad *thank you,* laying back down and rolling my face to the wall. She told me she loved me, then got up and walked away. When I think of this story now, I only think of her feelings, how isolated she must have felt in her life. I know how sad I am when I can't heal my own children's hurts.

My restless mind couldn't let it go. I wallowed and festered all day into the evening. Allie's brand-new beauty ruined, her sweet smell replaced by the sharp fumes of permanent marker and nail polish remover. The lost dream of her genie-like potential for making me cool, my baby sister's betrayal. I just kept working it all over in my head.

Maybe it had nothing to do with the doll. Maybe this was about the living, breathing love I'd lost when Loyd killed CC. Maybe it was about the fact that nobody but Jesse and I knew, that nobody talked about her, that forgetting her was required. I had nothing of CC to keep. She had loved me and now she didn't exist. She was silence. So maybe my voice was scream- ing out about something, anything, to make myself heard. Or maybe I'm overthinking it. I was probably just a shallow little brat.

Of course I didn't let it go. I got up in the middle of the night and snuck to the bathroom to get the nail polish remover. I tried to finish the job myself, carefully touching a Q-tip to that last black mark, ignoring Mom's good advice. Of course I swiped away a third of the doll's left eye. I started school that year without a Cabbage Patch, without a bike, without a dog. The same old fatherless loser as the year before, only now I walked alone because Jesse rode ahead with his friends, on his new bike.

Like most kids, I got swept up in the space shuttle *Challenger.* All fall we learned about the mission in school and I fell in love with Christa McAuliffe. I was always falling in love with teachers, playing out fantasies in my head where a favorite teacher would see something in me, something so special they'd decide to adopt me. Reading about the Teacher in Space program, it made perfect sense to me that Christa McAuliffe was quali- fied to go into space just because she was a really good teacher. I had little interest in space or astronauts. My *Challenger* curiosity was purely about my teacher crush. My adoption scenario for Christa McAuliffe was pretty elaborate and involved me winning some sort of school writing contest where I got to meet her, sometimes on TV. The whole nation watching as the first teacher in space met the child she'd adopt as soon as she returned from her mission.

I was sitting on the gym floor with my legs crossed, in a position our principal called *Indian style*, when I watched the *Challenger* launch. I didn't mind that the floor was cold and hard. Teachers had rolled out metal carts with televisions on them, extension cords running out in all directions, and the whole school was clustered around them in little islands of excitement. The *Challenger* exploded seventy-three seconds into launch, fire and pieces falling off into the Atlantic as the teachers rushed to switch off the TVs. I was still holding Christa McAuliffe's newsprint picture in my hand as we walked, single file, back to class. It felt like a personal loss, the teacher with the sweet smile, the teacher who was supposed to go to space.

steelhead

MOM HAD A BAD FEELING about our summer visit to Packwood. Loyd hadn't been in AA for a while and his voice over the phone had that wiry energy that came before trouble. It didn't help when he showed up to get us. He had the wrong sort of light in his eyes, a sore on the corner of his mouth, and his left arm in a plaster cast. The cast was clean and crisp, a bad sign. It wasn't the injury, or even that history taught Mom intoxication was likely the cause of the injury. It was the freshness of the cast, bright like bone growing on the outside of his skin. Newness meant a recent fight, suggested he was currently using. But this is how Mom lived with Loyd. She looked him in the face, tried to puzzle out the clues. She stared and searched, but when you love somebody it can be hard to actually see them. And life always kept coming, whether Loyd was using or not.

Sometimes, when I lie awake in the early morning re-watching the movie of my life, I beg Mom's character not to let her children go to Packwood. I always got a bad feeling at the start of "Little Red Riding Hood." I knew how fairy tales go and she's a little girl walking into a dark wood alone and I just wanted to yell at her—*don't go!* That's what it felt like at the start of that summer. Like we all knew it was a bad idea but also sort of meant to be. Kids visit their dad in summer and whatever happens, that's their story. Little Red will always skip into the forest and the wolf will always eat her. She'll emerge from the wood older and wiser and less carefree.

Turns out Loyd didn't have a house or a trailer in Packwood. He was squatting in the Gifford Pinchot National Forest. When he'd told Mom he had a great place in the woods, he wasn't lying. The place was amazing. It was also a tent. An army surplus tent he'd picked up at the giant Yard Birds in Chehalis. He called our home in Packwood "Camp," because it looked like a miniature logging camp. The first time I saw Camp, I knew it was enchanted and dangerous. Like entering the fairy kingdom.

Camp was the start of a new sort of housing for Loyd. He'd create similar homesteads in the years to follow. Usually, he'd start with a cast-off camp trailer, but in this case it was a tent. He'd integrate the basic shelter with lean-tos and rough structures of salvaged lumber, timber he harvested, and other collected materials. Each had its own charm but I loved Loyd's place in Packwood best of all the homes he ever made.

Camp was a child's fantasy. Deep in a lovely dark wood, shaded by conifers, and set about fifty feet back from the bank of a wide stream of rushing mountain runoff. I could imagine Paul Bunyan and Babe the Blue Ox sitting down to eat with us, could see Sleeping Beauty dancing in the surrounding trees with her animal friends. I was a child and wanted magic to be real. Camp made it easy to believe.

The tent sat farthest from the creek. It was made of green canvas and had the smallest woodstove I'd ever seen, with a pipe chimney sticking out through a hole on top. Right away I was worried about a woodstove in a tent but Loyd told me it was made for that, *same kind the army uses! This one coulda been in a war, who knows?* The first time I stepped into the tent I was sure some magic was at play because it seemed impossibly big on the inside. There were two small cots for us kids and a larger mattress on the ground for Dad and Linda. We each had two stacked milk crates for our things. In front of the woodstove was a folding card table with two chairs. The tent smelled musty and metallic, like rust.

When I walked out of the tent and turned toward the creek, I was in the kitchen. It was framed up with timbers from the surrounding forest. I could see each stroke of the ax Loyd used to clear the bark, splitting it off downward on every pole. Blue tarps hung, taut and neat, across the upper frame to create a roof and clear plastic sheeting was mounted in rolls along the perimeter to be let down as walls if it got to raining too hard. A light blue carpet remnant spread out under the entire kitchen area so it didn't have a dirt floor.

Mainly the kitchen was a wide countertop, about twelve feet long, of salvaged plywood. Linda had it organized. There was a propane camp stove, a couple of plastic washbasins, a dish drainer, and a big wooden cutting board. A frying pan, saucepan, and soup pot hung from nails along one end. Three large ice chests under the counter stored paper towels, coffee filters, saltine crackers, cereal, and bread. Anything that needed protection from animals and damp but didn't require refrigeration. Wood fruit crates were stacked and nailed as cupboards along the back edge of the counter. They held our dishes and other things that could be left out like cans of soup and chili, cooking oil, Crisco, jars of jam and peanut butter, and ketchup.

Buckets sat upside down on a dishtowel to dry, always ready to gather water to boil for dishes and drinking. But Jesse and I often drank straight from the clear creek, down on our bellies on the bank, faces in cold water. Our refrigerator was just an ice chest sunk directly into the stream. The top stood above the water line so we could reach in for milk, cheese, or bologna without getting our hands wet. Loyd kept beer nestled into the rocky shallow of the creek to stay cold.

Our living room was a big firepit surrounded by log bits and stumps as chairs. We sat around that fire most nights, watching it burn down until our eyes grew heavy and we dropped off, one by one, to the tent, stopping to say goodnight and give Dad a kiss on the way. Loyd was always the last one up, putting the fire out safely before he slept.

That first day, while Jesse and Loyd were horsing around, I went to the tent to unpack. I pulled my two milk crates closer to my cot, so I could use the tops as bedside tables. Sitting alone I took each shirt, pair of shorts, pants, underwear, socks, from my bag and refolded them into their new place. I tried to organize it, socks and underwear together, t-shirts and tank tops together, pants and shorts together, like Mom did. I'd brought three books with me and put them on top of the crate nearest my bed, my toothbrush on the opposite crate. Putting my things in order helped settle my nerves. All the way to Packwood, as I held my pillow close to my body in the car, I felt the familiar joy and anxiety of stepping onto the path into Loyd's world.

Loyd had a bunch of friends in Packwood, mostly other unemployed guys who did day labor for cash or trade. The single guys spent their nights drinking and trying to pick up women. The family guys tended to keep more regular work. Loyd could never decide which he was. His best buddy in the family-man category was Richard, a large, cheerful man with a red-headed wife and a few kids, all boys if I recall. Most of Loyd's single friends circled around a guy called Tom.

Tom was built like Loyd, wiry and a little short. But he was a bit taller and more bulky. He had hair the color of a paper sack and women seemed to find him handsome, but his face reminded me of a hyena. I knew from the *Weekly Reader*s I got at school that hyenas couldn't be trusted. Even if they didn't look like much, they could tear you apart in no time and smile while doing it. I was careful never to turn my back on Tom. I didn't accept treats from him or react to his jokes. Mom taught me a few ways to avoid advances from grown-up men. First time I met Tom I sensed he was a man who'd make them.

Tom lived in a string of clapboard cottages, probably built to house crews back during the logging boom. There were six or eight cabins housing out-of-work loggers or millworkers in the same three-room floor plan. Kitchen open to sitting area, a bedroom you had to walk through to get to the tiny bathroom. The cabins all shared the same long patch of grass with a horseshoe pitch and slanting badminton net off to the side. Loyd and his friends gathered at Tom's often. They'd banish us outside to play while the adults holed up inside to party. We'd wander in and out of the cottages, beg for snacks or maybe score a can of pop to pass around.

Sometimes the adults would organize a badminton or horseshoe tour-nament. Mostly men played while the women sat in the grass or on the little porches smoking and calling out. I loved watching Loyd play horseshoes. He'd holler for me when it was his turn so I could stop whatever I was doing and run over to cheer. *Tina Marie, it's almost my turn. Hurry up, squirt, Daddy needs his good luck charm!* When Loyd wound up to throw a horseshoe, his body reminded me of a ballerina, though I had the sense never to tell him that. He had a sort of intrinsic physical grace. Falling a tree or throwing a football, his body was somehow perfectly aligned with his mind, I don't know how else to describe it. When Loyd was doing something physical, he often reminded me of a sculpture. Something meant to be observed. He'd put one foot behind him, bend his right arm, and hold the horseshoe to his face, eyes peering through to the pitch. His fingertips met at the bottom of the horseshoe, pointing up to God. Every muscle stood to show itself—in his face, his arms, his legs. When he paused like that before throwing, he looked like a pencil sketch meant to be a study in lines. Both hands would swing out behind him and the left would stay back there while the right launched ahead, sending the horseshoe flying, his hips moving forward with it. Flawless motion as organic as any force of nature.

Sunny mornings in Packwood we might go pick huckleberries or blackberries then sell them to a man at the fruit stand. If we had a good haul Loyd might take us for ice cream or let us pick a candy at the market. We spent lots of time with Aunt Rainy that summer. Our cousins were younger than us but we still liked going to their house to play. They lived in a manufactured home that seemed like the height of stability. Aunt Rainy's house had a wide deck, a separate TV room for the kids, and lots of toys. She made all our meals and didn't give us chores, only expected us to stay out of her hair. We'd stay there for a day or two and we didn't mind but were always excited to go back to Loyd, Linda, and Camp.

We were at Rainy's one hot afternoon, running in the sprinkler, when Loyd pulled up and hollered at us to get in the car. He was electric. I always thought of the sparkle in Loyd's eyes as a warm light, like the twinkling of Christmas bulbs. But this time it was different, like the flickering harsh of tube lights overhead at the gas station. Pretty sure Aunt Rainy noticed, too, because she got worried.

Somethin' got you riled up, Bro? She asked. They only ever called each other *Bro* or *Sis*. Loyd didn't respond to her, just barked at Jesse and me.

Giddyup, let's get a move on! Rainy tried to stall him, get him to *sit down, share a smoke, shoot the shit,* but he was in a hurry. She asked if maybe he should *leave the rug rats here, keep 'em out from underfoot?* Loyd said Linda was making us dinner. He was buzzing. I could see energy, little bolts of lightening, sparking off him. Rainy told us to go get dressed but he said there wasn't time, said we could just sit on a towel. We piled in, scrunched together on the one towel Loyd borrowed, and took off. I asked where Linda was and he said she was waiting for us to pick her up at Tom's. We soaked through the towel right away. It was a hot day but the water didn't even have time to evaporate from my skin before we got to Tom's.

On the way, I noticed Richard's red-headed family at the market that sat right across the highway from the row of cabins. Richard was easy to spot around town because he drove a dark green, classic Ford truck. There was something about him, the way he opened doors for his wife and was always packing one of his kids, that made me like him. He was friendly but gave me space. His wife was round and very kind to me. She'd given her bright rosy hair and face to all their children and I felt an envy toward those kids that I couldn't make sense of. I saw the whole ruddy clan spilling out of their truck and heading into the store, their bright heads bobbing along, just as we turned into the short lane to Tom's cabin.

Our rusting, powder blue Pinto pulled to a gravel-spewing stop just down the row from Tom's. You'd think Loyd had been stung by a bee, the way he jumped out of the car. He motioned to us, index finger over his lips, to follow as he skirted around the cinder-block foundation of Tom's cabin, stopping to listen and peek in each window.

We followed at a safe distance. A safe distance. We'd developed interior mechanisms to gauge this in any situation. It seems simple. What's the farthest I can keep from him without igniting his temper? But there were always so many variables to factor in. I often found myself still gathering data in that moment when a solution became critical.

Loyd approached the last window. It was open. Tiny blue flowers were printed on the cotton curtain, which was hanging partially outside, drifting in the warm breeze. Scratching softly against the white peeling paint of the siding, it made peaceful sounds. Looking at that curtain made me think of a commercial for fabric softener. Loyd lifted the curtain to peek inside. I heard quick, huffing sounds float out toward me. Loyd's face was joyful, his fluorescent lights screaming bright. He waved his hand to hurry us closer.

I can see now how it all pieced together in his mind, how careful his planning was. He yanked back that curtain like an excited game-show host and behind curtain number one were Linda and Tom. Loyd gave the scene a few seconds before he hollered out.

Look kids! Look at what your mother's doing!

I know she wasn't technically our mother. She was our stepmother, in spirit if no longer in law. But she was ours. She'd traded in a brighter, cleaner life and become our family. Now she was naked, flushed, and sweaty on Tom's bed. Now Tom was naked on top of her, his narrow hips between her legs. Now her eyes found my face but didn't seem to see me. Her eyes looked like they'd burst open and released everything they once held.

This image is suspended. Nothing can move. Not her eyes, empty and faraway, or my own. My eyes have become heavy, beyond my strength to move. And I want to move them. Anywhere but here.

I felt a rush in my head. I could hear the first sign of motion before time started again. I knew the sound of violence. In that held breath, that frozen, hot summer day, I knew to fear what was coming. Warm energy started in my core and ran up and down through the center of my body, preparing me.

It was not in Loyd's voice or the breathless panting from Tom and Linda. Violence has a presence. It takes up space, makes its own noise. For me, it was a white noise only I could hear. Like my body's reaction to the sound of the sea in my ears, the hair on the back of my neck stood on end and I shivered before something more powerful than me. Something that could sweep me away.

Tom withdrew from Linda, jumped up in front of these two children he'd told to call him *Uncle Tom*. Now Uncle Tom looked at us through the window, determined and full of malice. I was on my tiptoes, my palms wrapped on the bottom of the window frame to hold me up. He pulled a pair of tattered canvas cutoffs over his shrinking erection and screamed at Loyd.

I'm gonna kill you! But he seemed afraid. Everyone knew my dad was a fighter.

Loyd looked like he'd won a contest and had a prize to claim as he ran around the corner to meet Tom at the front door. He started up the three porch stairs just as Tom burst out the door. From the second stair Loyd lunged upward and got in the first punch. He swung his heavy left arm, still in the dirty gray cast, at Tom's mouth. I heard contact, the wet push of air Tom expelled. Blood spread bright red over the plaster wrist area of Loyd's cast. I turned and ran away.

I ran so fast I could feel my colors smearing out behind me. I crossed the highway without looking both ways. A car honked at me and I slowed at the stab of shame I felt. My mom taught me better than to run into traffic. Once across, I erupted into the market, swimsuit still wet, hair clinging together in stringy clumps, looking for Richard's family. I yelled out before I could even see them.

Help! Tom's hitting my daddy!

Then Richard was in front of me. He knelt down, put his hands on my shoulders, and asked where my dad was. I pulled his hand and led him outside, pointed across the highway, and sniffled out that he was at Tom's.

Richard jumped in his truck, backed up, turned sharp, and drove off toward the cottages. I stood in the parking lot, Richard's wife wiping my face with her sleeve. I knew there was snot mixed with my tears and I felt ashamed again. I was mad at Loyd for making me get snot on somebody else's mother. But I also basked in her attention, loved her soft arms around me, the way she smelled like Tide and cookies, and the way her kids looked at me like I was taking something that belonged to them. I see now that I've burned a lot of energy since then trying to be like her, the mother everyone wants.

Eventually the green truck came back with Jesse on the bench seat. He was pushed up against the passenger door. I thought he was so strong and brave. He always stayed, never ran and hid. His face showed no sign of tears. I don't think I ever saw my brother cry. He's seen me cry so much he might consider an aspect of my personality.

Richard took us back to Aunt Rainy. Someone must've called her because she was expecting us and she was gentle with us, soft. Jesse and I didn't talk about what we'd seen, to each other or our aunt. No use. We didn't see Loyd for a couple more days. I wondered where he was, if Linda was with him, what they were doing. I wondered if my mom knew what happened, what she would do if she did.

Finally, Loyd came to take us back to Camp. He had fading bruises on his face but said Tom looked worse. I wanted to know exactly what happened after I ran away, but didn't ask. I only managed to spit out a few words.

But Daddy, I saw blood on you!

Just saying it out loud got me crying. Loyd said that was no big deal, that he only had blood on him because his first swing hit Tom square in the mouth and his front tooth sliced right into the thumb Loyd had sticking out of the cast. *But don't worry, honey.* He chuckled, touched by my concern. *Daddy got the better of him, right Jess?* My brother gave a forced half smile to confirm Loyd's story. I inspected the cast, turning his arm over with my hands. The blood had dried a rusty brown on the plaster. There was a thick scab on the top of his thumb. I asked him if it hurt. He gave a familiar answer. *Sweetheart, if I ain't hurtin', I ain't livin'.*

Linda wasn't at Camp when we got back. I asked where she was. When I'd seen her on Tom's bed, I felt betrayed. Not for Loyd but for myself. I was a kid but I already knew Linda had plenty of good reasons to betray Loyd. But I was also self-centered enough to wonder why she didn't think of me before getting in Tom's bed. It felt like she'd made a choice to be separated from us.

Dad told us Linda would be away for a few days or so. He tried to explain what happened, said they'd been at Tom's playing cards with the whole gang when Linda got a real bad headache. Tom brought her aspirin except it wasn't aspirin. It was something that made her sleepy and unable to stand. Now she felt bad about the whole thing so she was taking some time to herself. Loyd didn't try to explain his own behavior.

Camp was strange without Linda. I hadn't been able to sleep well since I'd seen her and Tom together. What haunted me wasn't Tom's violent threat or even his nudity, though that image shocked me for sure. I'd never seen that part of a grown man before and seeing those two bodies like that changed something in me. But it was Linda's eyes I saw when I tried to sleep at night. They were dark and empty, like someone took out her eyes and replaced them with the glass eyes of a doll. There were forces shaping our story that I didn't see back then. I couldn't know that Loyd and Linda were users of more than alcohol and funny cigarettes. I couldn't know that meth labs were spreading across Loyd's territory about as fast as sawmills and timber outfits were disappearing. What I did know was that some evil force had taken Linda's eyes and that whatever controlled her body that afternoon, it wasn't Linda.

Linda had shaped our days, kept the rhythm of Camp. Preparing meals, cleaning up, planning trips to town to get groceries for more meals. I woke each morning to the smell of coffee she brewed, knew it was almost dinner when I smelled onions frying, heard pots and pans knocking. Without her we ate mostly out of cans or boxes. Cereal, hot dogs, chicken noodle soup. Loyd bought a Gallo salami chub, which I considered fancy because it said *Italian* on the label. He let us cut chunks off ourselves with his pocketknife and I loved peeling away the dusty white casing, letting it curl into my lap as I worked at it. It was a messy process but Loyd didn't mind. He was trying to make it seem fun. Like we were getting away with something.

We ran to town one day because Loyd needed more Campho-Phenique. I came to associate the medicinal eucalyptus smell with my dad because he was often fighting cold sores. Going to town was more fun without Linda. Jesse and I got to pick out most of what went into our grocery cart and didn't have to fold laundry at the Laundromat. We just pulled it from the dryer and threw it in a bag. That day we also needed to fill the propane tank and make our weekly call to Mom from the pay phone outside the gas station.

I knew something was off as we pulled up back at Camp. The lines of the tent were wrong. I hadn't yet taken in the whole scene but I felt my spine straighten, sparks run up my neck and behind my ears. The tent was listing. I forced my eyes from it and saw that all the lines were wrong, the geometry of Camp was completely off-kilter.

A bright yellow shirt was hanging, hooked on top of one of the poles that had supported our kitchen roof but was now leaning toward the ground. It was the optimistic, sunny shirt of a child. I didn't see it as mine, I felt so tired. That yellow pushed through my eyes and burned a high-pitched squeal in my ears. The silent scream increased in volume, bouncing back at me like an echo from the off-balance tilt of Camp, as we slowly drove closer.

From the backseat I could see that all the support beams leaned one way or another. Our clothes were sprinkled around, on the ground or hanging from whatever snagged them as they were thrown. Blue tarp bunched on the ground instead of soaring over our heads on lumber pillars, shielding us from sun and rain. Loyd hit the brakes and my body lurched forward. He told us to stay in the car and jumped out so fast you'd think he was late for an appointment. He burned too, like the shirt. He lit up with anger and the squeal got louder. I wanted to get out with him.

But Daddy . . .

STAY in the car! It was the voice I knew better than to question. I rolled down the passenger window and lifted my body out for a better view, my butt on the window frame, left arm stretched across the sun-warmed roof of the car for balance. My coloring book was open and face down in the dirt. Socks and underwear, pots and pans. All of our things were tossed around like trash. Loyd walked through, picking things up and shaking the dirt off. I saw a few cans of soup on the ground and thought of the cold food in our creek fridge. I yelled from the car.

Daddy . . . what about my jar of pickles? Loyd went to the creek and hollered back to me.

They're fine, honey! The suckers didn't find our fridge! That pleased him, like he'd outsmarted them or something. He whooped and laughed and somehow that made the screeching stop. Now it was just the quiet of Camp, the smell of the forest, the singing of birds, the rush of the creek. Loyd came back to the car and said we could get out. Whoever did it was long gone.

I'm not sure the vocabulary exists to explain what that felt like. To see the things we used every day—clothes we wore, food we ate, pans we cooked with—all strewn about and dusty. To see the shelter that housed us no longer standing tall. Jesse's Star Wars bedsheet tossed aside, draped over the undergrowth of wild salal, floating like a ghost. And to know it was all done on purpose, that we were the targets. Grown men, three to five I'm sure, based on Tom's usual posse, had stomped on my sleeping cot until it broke. To know that three to five grown men had opened my coveted smelly markers and flung them out, three to five grown men had ripped pages from my copy of *Reader's Digest Condensed Books*, Volume 4, which I'd begged Mom to buy me at Salvation Army and considered classy because of its handsome green cloth cover. Three to five grown men tore those pages out and spread them across Camp, mixed with all the other things they'd smashed or slashed just to make their point.

I waded through the ruin of Camp aware of a new sort of danger. Loyd's monster was familiar and felt manageable. I thought I'd always be able to slash my way out of the belly of his wolf. Of course that's silly but that's how children think. No matter how much independent experience is packed into an eleven-year-old life, no matter how old her soul, she's still a child.

This vandalism, this demolition of our enchanted place, was a whole new violence. New monsters had come for us. Not one wolf but an entire pack and none of them loved me. I believed one of them actually hated me because I'd looked him in the eye at his moment of shame. I'd seen him exposed and met his gaze without looking away. I remembered that stranger in front of the Kingdom Hall back in Morton and how he told me that looking into an animal's eyes invites attack.

Tom had come with his pack to violate and terrorize us. To turn our belongings into trash. He'd transformed the home our dad built for us into a junk heap and a warning. *You are not safe here.* Three to five wolves would return and not even children would be spared. Dad told us to pack up. We gathered what we'd brought from Mom's, as much as we could find, and went back to Aunt Rainy's.

That night, Loyd called Mom from Aunt Rainy's house. They talked for a while, then she wanted to hear our voices. She talked to Jesse first, then me. I twisted the curly phone cord around my fingers, one at a time, turning it hard until the circulation was cut off. I watched my finger turn white and held the pressure as long as I could stand before moving on to the next. Switching hands to maintain balance. Mom asked if I was OK. I told her I was. She knew about what happened to Camp but I don't think anyone told her about Linda, Tom, and the fight. I wasn't about to add to her worry. She said she missed us and thought we should come home a little early. I told her that was a good idea. Dad talked with us, too. He said we should head back to Mom's since Camp wasn't safe. That maybe even Packwood wasn't safe for us. I worried Packwood wasn't safe for Loyd, either. And I felt guilty because I was glad to go.

Before we left, Loyd took us to Packwood Lake. Jesse and I had heard of the lake with an island of trees in its center and asked Loyd to take us earlier that summer. But he said we had to earn it. You couldn't just drive to the lake. It was about a five-mile hike in. Loyd often poked fun at our life in *the Big City*. He said we might not be able to handle the long walk and he didn't want to pack any whining kids. But after everything that happened, he decided to take us.

We made a picnic of bologna sandwiches on white bread with mayo and American cheese, potato chips, and beer for Loyd. Jesse and I carried the old Coleman ice chest the whole time. It had a dark green aluminum shell with a silver rotating clasp on front and handles that rested into square indents on either side. We held it between us, one handle in my left hand, one in his right, our bodies leaning outward as we walked. Every so often we'd switch sides, when we couldn't stand the way the rounded metal slid from our sweaty palms to dig into our fingers. We swapped without speaking, the decision sent along the ice chest like electricity. We packed it all the way without complaining.

Every step brought another miracle. I was mostly a child of sidewalks. At Mom's I walked to and from school, to DeHart's market for dime boxes of Lemonheads or cigarettes, Mom's handwritten note paper-clipped to the cash. I walked to the Chenowith Rim Apartments to see my friends, running my fingers along chain-link as I went. Though I always lived in or near the woods with Loyd, this was my first real nature hike. I'd heard you could see Goat Rocks from the lake and was hoping to find some of the mountain goats said to climb the peaks. Layers of fallen pine needles made the path soft under my feet and the sun passing through the canopy created a green glow that colored my brother's face beautiful. We climbed gently through old-growth western red cedar and Doug fir. Dogwood, salmon-berry, and Oregon grape grew close to the path. The air was rich in animal chatter and the sweet smell of warm cedar. The whole forest sang and twin-kled. Everything was talking, gentle, to everything else.

When we heard flowing water Loyd said we were almost there. I could see bits of lake through gaps in the trees. The birdsong shifted at the thresh-old to a small clearing. I felt the cooling aura of the creek before I saw it. Loyd said it was fed by Old Snowy Mountain and I liked the sound of that. I heard slapping and splashing. When I turned toward the racket, I saw that a wide spot in the creek was crowded with large bright fish, so many they couldn't help but touch. Orange backs, green tails, all pushing together. Bright midday sun bounced off them, they made their own light. Colorful glare, the noisy clatter of their shoving, the fish seemed to erupt before us. It was a sudden, jarring display of life.

I didn't speak or even look at Jesse, but we communicated. We both dropped the ice chest at the same instant. It hit the ground, handles hitting the sides with a sharp clang, like a bell that invited us into the dream of the salmon. We waded in, shin-deep in writhing madness. We had no respect for the fish, only wanted to get our hands on the flopping, gleaming creatures.

At first I just touched them. Felt them against my shins, extended my arms out to run my fingertips over greasy, rough scales. Then, I grabbed. Wrapped my fingers around fish, one after another, working up courage to grasp and pull. When I thought I'd found the biggest, I lifted him up in my hands like I pictured a bear might. It was important to imagine the fish was male. I couldn't let myself trouble a fish mother. I snuck a glance at Jesse, hoping I'd caught a larger fish.

I held him close, under my armpit. He was strong and slippery but there was a roughness to his scales I hadn't expected. Texture made him more real to me, more complicated. I lifted him away from my body, suspended him in warm summer air, eye to eye. I caused the sun to glint off his body in this new way. I created the streams of water that fell away from him. I exposed him to this new reality. I knew he'd come home after a long journey. Growing up in the Pacific Northwest means growing up in the land of sea-migrating fish. I'd been learning about the life cycle of salmon, the Jesus-like sacrifice they make of their bodies, since kindergarten. He was a warrior. He'd survived sharks and saltwater and an impossible uphill swim to be plucked from the water here, in the final stage of his mission, by a girl in orange-sherbet gym shorts. A girl child with ratty blond hair pulled back in a two-day ponytail and an elbow scraped and scabbing over from tripping on a root in the woods.

He fought and he was mighty but I was stronger. A white scar ran along his brow. His peeling scales, ragged tail, and cloudy eyes were signs of decay. Still, he was beautiful. I'd never held something so bursting. Red and orange with green face and tail, his colors seemed impossible. His colors were falling away from him.

Loyd hollered his approval and I celebrated my power over the creature, who I'd come to think of as the King of Salmon. Later, I'd realize these were likely steelhead. And that feels right to me because steel is strong. Feels like that emphasizes the girl's courage in this story. I want her to be brave.

The steelhead's body of muscle was tugging away from me, urged to complete his biological duty before dying. I wished I could give him some of my energy, my youth, the magic children are sometimes aware they possess. I wanted to grant him longer life and more glory. More slicing through clear streams with pebble beds. My arms grew tired so I pulled him close to my chest, the scab on my elbow crackling as it was forced to bend. He was running out of fight and that made me sad.

The lessons of every fish hatchery field trip felt like injustice to me. It wasn't fair that he should live only to fertilize eggs then die. As a child, I deeply questioned the story of Jesus. It made no sense. If I was Jesus, I just wouldn't show up for the terrible chores God gave me. I wouldn't walk to my own crucifixion carrying my own cross. Did a salmon never stray from his predetermined path? What if a steelhead never returned home because she liked the wide-open expanse and strange, beautiful creatures of the sea? If I could just whisper the right words in his fish ear, which I searched for but could not find, maybe I could tell him another story. A story where he makes his own fate. It was a secret I'd wonder about in the years to come, how to step out of the story written for me.

But in that moment, I also wanted to eat him. To smash his head, slice open his body, remove the unwanted parts with a sharp tool. I didn't like eating fish but I wanted to be able to say we'd eaten the King of Salmon, the fish I'd caught with my bare hands like a caveman. The one I held tight in my girl fingers and lifted with my spaghetti arms as the stream ran off his body and down mine, dripping off my elbows to return to itself.

I asked Loyd if we could eat him, if we wanted. Loyd said none of these fish were good to eat. All they were good for now was making babies and dying. My compassion stirred again. The fish was relaxing in my arms. I shared a look with Jesse. We both reveled in the power of our opposable thumbs. We could dash these fish against the rocks, we could slash them open, we could set them free. Loyd said we'd better get a move on.

I loved the steelhead in my hands and I loved them all. Kissing his side, I whispered a goodbye to the ear I never found but felt sure existed. I released him back to the stream. I felt a swelling in my throat, the familiar lump that appeared when we started or ended our time with Loyd. I'd always thought of it as a friendly helper, a physical reaction that stopped confusing emotion from overtaking me. Leaving a parent meant I had to be strong for them. Expressing grief would only make it harder.

I'd held the steelhead in my hands and I'd let him go. That's what Loyd taught me. Love means leaving and being left. Love is separation and loss. If you love something, set it free. To splash through crisp mountain runoff. To swim and spawn. To gleam in the sun.

(the worst thing)

ONE NIGHT IN THE TIME BETWEEN, while we lived in Camp without Linda, I bent to kiss my dad goodnight and he forced his tongue in my mouth.

(I should probably say more about the worst thing)

Here's the deal. I've thought a lot about that night Loyd tried to kiss me like that. I don't want you to think it was the end of my innocence or anything because that wouldn't be exactly true. I don't think I ever had innocence like that. The innocence we imagine for children. I wish I could say I was a stranger to this sort of thing but Loyd was not the first grown man to approach me in that way.

By the time I stepped into Loyd's enchanted forest that summer, I already knew the shame of unwanted touch and the guilt of being manipulated into my own abuse. I'd learned to dodge adult men and teenage boys. Through personal experience and whispers between cousins, aunts, my mother, I understood the costs of being a pretty or well-kept little girl. And I was familiar with the economy of abuse. It's a system set up so I'd never consider myself a victim because I knew another girl who was hurt worse, another at a younger age, and another whose older brother was trained to take up where her father left off so her body hardly had rest. I knew stories so scary that my own life, pierced with grimy episodes that were painful, but that I got up and walked away from, seemed normal.

But all that was in my other life, my life with a single mom forced to let us raise ourselves much of the time. In Packwood I was with my dad. Loyd was the one man I had faith would never try that stuff. Once that faith was lost, so was my devotion to my dad. I no longer felt the pull to be his daughter.

Before the kiss, Loyd was like the sun to me. I could feel his warmth and the tug of his gravity from far away. I was nourished by his glow. Distance didn't erase the feeling that he was with me, whatever I did. I could always sense the force that kept us in one another's orbit. Now that weight was gone, it was cold, and I drifted. Many children of trauma have this ability to cut the tether attaching them to another person in an instant.

This was the moment I started calling him *Loyd* in my head. Before the kiss he'd always been *Daddy*. There are other men I've called family, then never spoken to again. Family connections, both good and bad, are part of the price I paid for my ticket out of generational poverty. I've seen my uncle begging for bottles and cans in front of Safeway and kept driving. An older cousin so haunted my childhood that today, if I see him the grocery store, I pretend I don't know who he is. I've cut ties with much of my genetic family. Loyd was the one that hurt the most. I think he knew, too. Right in that moment he could tell he'd lost me.

Jesse, Loyd, and I sat around the firepit late that night. My brother and I had an unspoken competition to see who could stay up latest. Jesse usually won. On that night I won, Jesse went to bed first.

Not long after, I started drowsing as I sat there on a warm stump. My body drifted toward the heat of the embers. I caught myself and pulled back. I looked across at Loyd in the glow. His eyes were on the dying fire, arms crossed over his chest against the chill. Right leg crossed over left knee, gold and white Oly can in his left hand. His face looked golden, bathed in firelight. I got up and crossed over to him.

Night, Daddy.

Goin' to sleep honey?

Yeah, gonna fall in the fire. And I leaned my fire-warmed face toward him, like every night. Drew my lips to his cheek for a quick peck, like always. As long as memory. But this was not like every night. Loyd put his right hand on the back of my head, twisted my face toward his, held my head in place, and forced his tongue into my mouth. He tasted like beer and cigarettes.

Then I was awake. I twisted my neck and pulled my body away. I hauled out the imaginary tool belt that I normally put away when I was with Loyd. I hadn't expected this from him but I knew what to do. I stood, as tall as I could just out of his reach, and faced him.

For a brief moment he just looked at me, his face open to what might come next. It was like he was gauging my reaction, waiting to see if I was game. Like he'd extended an invitation. It occurred to me he might wonder if I was already trained by some other man. It occurred to me he might know children who were.

I could've imagined it and memory is a funny thing, but I think the next moment was one of complete, clear communication without words. I faced him the way you're taught to face a bear or a cougar. I made myself as big as I could and tried to seem unafraid. Predators can smell fear.

That old trusted line of electricity ran up my spine, out through the top of my head, and touched the stars above. I always thought of it as a special power that came to me when the wolf was near. This time, Loyd could sense it, too. He hung his head like a dog. He didn't come toward me. He didn't get angry. I didn't hear the rushing white noise of violence approaching. Instead, Loyd took three slow, wet breaths. He wiped tears from his eyes and made another long, snorting inhale.

Before he could speak, I turned my back and walked away. I left him there with himself, as my mother had before me. I walked, slow and deliberate. I didn't want to look like I was running away. Wolves get more hungry when they chase. I was desperate to be calm, not to behave like prey.

I went to bed but didn't sleep. I curled up and coached myself that I must scream and wake Jesse if Loyd came for me again. That I must not be silent if that happened. I knew how hard it could be to find my voice in moments like that. And though I had survived worse at the hands of other wolves, there was singular horror for me in allowing myself to be torn apart by this one, my own dad.

He didn't come for me. Sometimes, I wish he'd tried again and that I'd found the courage to wake my brother. Because then the little girl would've had a witness to her pain. But that didn't happen so the girl is alone. For so many years she is alone in that night.

I never spoke with Loyd about that kiss and he never tried anything like that with me again. When I was younger, I had a fantasy that Loyd had other kids with other moms. That maybe his migrations were set up to make time for all his families. I'd dream of meeting these secret siblings and finding myself in them. Now I worried for them. I hoped I was the only girl.

His tongue wasn't the worst violation. It was his hand. His hand held me still, forced me into the position that allowed for his tongue. The movements of his hand felt calculated, suggested a level of planning. Even if it only took seconds, this felt like it doubled or tripled the violation because it meant he looked at me *that way*. He looked at me and thought of jabbing his tongue into my mouth.

Strange thing is, I never felt more like Loyd than I did when I faced him down that night. When I stood there looking in his eyes, I could see Loyd on Tom's porch, shoulders back, chest forward. I knew I looked like a fighter. I guess what I mean to say is that I think, in some ways, Loyd had given me the ferocity I needed to defy him. In this moment, and in others to come. Funny how our relationships with our parents are so like a labyrinth, how a father's lessons can turn in on him. How his love can trap his children.

❰ ❰ ❰

I considered not telling you about the worst thing. I've considered it when I should be sleeping or when I'm driving or scratching my dog behind her ears. I've wondered—why do I need to tell that part? What's the point? Is the story still true if I leave the kiss out?

❰ ❰ ❰

I think of Loyd as a storyteller. But it was Mom who taught me the importance of telling your own story, that there is power in telling. She began telling her stories in whispers. I think motherhood broke her silence. I think it was having a daughter. Raising a girl comes with its own set of moral stories. A whole canon of oral folklore exists, spoken by mothers and grandmothers and aunts, to keep girls safe.

I've only heard pieces of my mom's stories. Most mothers tell just enough to teach a lesson, afraid of how their daughters would look at them if they heard the whole truth. Mom leaked out bits of her stories as needed. When I was very young, only when it related to basic safety. *Stay quiet when your dad is mad. When I send you to your room, stay there. I know you can't sleep, pretend to be asleep.* As I grew older, she'd fill them out, make them more specific.

Leaving Loyd meant accepting help from her own family. And she comes from a family where generations of men and boys take what they want from generations of girls and women. And what they want is pretty much always the same thing. She told me stories and gave me strategies. Like a coach watching playback with her team. Women and girls live this way all the time, every day. Right now, as you read this, another mother is telling her daughter what my mom told me.

Don't sit on Grandpa's lap.

Don't get caught alone with Uncle Johnny.

Ken will try to tickle you—avoid it.

Act like your tummy hurts.

Act like you have to pee.

Act like you're going to throw up.

Actually throw up. Here, I'll show you how.

We tell stories to entertain and delight, to frighten and motivate. We also tell stories to instruct. To guide children, help them learn from our mistakes. Mom's early instructions might not seem like stories, but there was never a time I didn't understand they were. Stories she had survived. I could feel them in my own body. An inheritance.

Life with Mom was soaked in these kinds of stories. She tried to limit our contact with the men in her family but we were sometimes without housing. For the poor, life is constant negotiation with predators. Wolves are always glad to offer shelter to sheep. This deep ugliness I associated with the men in Mom's family helped me idealize Loyd. He got angry sometimes, lost his temper, hit people. I didn't really understand that was abuse. I hit Jesse when I was mad—it was a gray area. At least when I was with Loyd I didn't feel like a mouse in a forest full of owls.

But this moment in Packwood was no gray area. Loyd lost the sacred space I'd held for him. I feel guilty for thinking that kiss is the worst thing. Loyd beat, raped, and cheated on Mom and Linda. He thought these were the rights of a husband, to give them bruises and debt and STDs. He was never dependable when we needed a father. He laid a foundation of poverty under our childhood out of spite. These things are worse than this one momentary slip.

But I won't lie. For me, this was the worst thing. That kiss is the bad thing against which I measure all bad things. Never in my whole story, before or after, has anything desolated me like that kiss. I was helpless and hopeless and worthless and fatherless.

In a fairytale it might say, *he kissed her and time stopped.* Loyd did kiss me and time did stop and no revision can make that disappear. I could erase it from the yellow legal pad I've scrawled Loyd out on, but it wouldn't dissolve the worst thing. Time stopped and never started again. I know because I still visit that moment and see the girl frozen there.

My twenty-year-old self, my thirty-year-old self, all of my selves have returned to that stopped moment in Camp to walk around, consider the scene, look for clues, try to learn something. I want to trust that pain serves a purpose. I want to believe we can make something good from trauma. I can't change anything Loyd did so I want to find a way he gets to do those terrible things and still be a good man. Not just because I loved him, also because he's half of me. There is no reality in which I get a different father. If he's a monster, what does that make me?

Even now I go back to that cedar-scented summer night and the orange campfire casting its glow on the child and her dad. She's glaring at him for the first time in her life. Her face isn't childlike, though she was still ten just weeks before. Her face isn't sad or pleading or wishful. She does not look afraid. She looks pissed and she's letting him know. She resembles him even more when her face is washed over in raw, ragged anger. Looking at her eyes, I see the sharp gleam, a suggestion she might transform into her own wolf. I step up close, bend down to look at her hate-filled face, and ask myself, *why? What's the lesson in this?*

My sixteen-year-old self will walk through the scene and find all the evidence she needs to fuel a righteous anger, to convict her father and lock him away. My twenty-year-old self, when she's pulled in against her will, walks through with her eyes closed and ears covered, pretending. My thirty-year-old self begins to look with forensic curiosity. Each self feels it in her body the same.

Now, my forty-year-old self walks through the kitchen to look in the tent at Jesse, asleep on his cot, blond head sweaty, that cowlick sticking straight up to heaven. Soon, he'll begin to look like a man in the making.

For now, nothing has changed for him. I look at the empty double mattress where Linda should be. Her absence is a force I can feel. Like a vacuum trying to suck my eleven-year-old self in.

I walk back over to the girl and I know she's afraid. She isn't sure her defiance will go unpunished. She's listening for the sound of violence. But her face doesn't show it. Her face is pure disgust. I want to do something for her but I know she'll face the wolf by herself. She has to, that's how she makes me. I have to leave her there, every time. There is nothing for her except to face this monster and many others in the years to come. So I can be made.

When I stand there with her, I think of the fairy tales she imagined in that forest. Stories teach us. I consider Little Red Riding Hood, Rapunzel, Sleeping Beauty. Stalked by a wolf, imprisoned, cursed then awakened with a kiss. Lessons in restricting each girl's freedom, limiting her movement. Narrowing her choices. Girls trapped in the middle of their own stories. In a tower, a glass coffin, the belly of a wolf.

And I consider the labyrinth of myth, built by Daedalus to trap the Minotaur at its center. The thing at the center of that labyrinth is always a monster, half-man, half-beast. And the beast has a magnetic power, it draws the hero inward. Maybe this metaphor doesn't work for me since I relate to the half-beast. My point is there's danger and evil at the center of the labyrinth. I don't want Loyd's kiss at my center. I don't want to keep tracing my story back to a monster.

There will always be times when the girl is sucked back into that infinite moment. The first time she kisses a boy from school, she's standing in Packwood with her dad's tongue in her mouth. Even when she buries the kiss, revises the history she tells herself, the kiss leaves its lingering stain. Through adolescence she'll flirt and enjoy the build-up, the tension before kissing, but she can find no pleasure in actual kissing because it's a time machine she can't control. That moment still has power over her today. If she thinks of it while she's jogging, she runs faster. If it comes to mind while she's washing dishes, she'll scrub harder.

Storytelling is a process of discovery. Telling like a journey. Though I might tell a story twice, the Tina who told it last time is not the Tina who tells it now. And though the story starts and ends at the same place, elements change each time. The story expands and contracts. I'm reshaping. Something of these evolutions stays with me. I'm changing with the story.

Storytelling is like walking a labyrinth. A labyrinth begins and ends at the same place each time. Like a seasonal migration. Though there are turns along the way and the path can feel ambiguous to the traveler, you always journey to the center and back. I can walk the path over and over but never have the same experience. A wolf roams the same territory but each migration is distinct. Each time it feels different. A labyrinth doesn't change but that doesn't mean the walker can't change. The act of migration changes her. Storytelling changes her.

Do you remember your first kiss? I'm sure you do. That's why this story wouldn't be true without the kiss. Some stories have nothing to teach us. Some just make us feel less alone. Maybe other children have kisses like that trapped in their bellies. Maybe they can walk with the girl through her labyrinth. And maybe there's something to be learned about survival. Maybe, with a story, the girl can free herself. I swallowed the kiss and kept it in my belly for thirty years. Maybe I can cut it out, as Little Red was cut from the belly of the wolf. Maybe time can start again.

Whenever I'm ambushed by the memory of the kiss, I imagine the steelhead. In that moment, I was powerful like the wolf. I could destroy the fish. Instead I lowered him gently to the stream, his home. Maybe I'm like the fish. Maybe Loyd plucked me from the water and nearly choked me out of life. But that's too simple. As I write this I look down at my hands and I see his hands. Sometimes, my anger has flashed and I've expected to see wiry hairs sprout from my own knuckles, for claws to erupt. These hands are half-wolf.

It's not exactly true to say that I didn't return to Loyd for a couple of summers. Because part of me never left Packwood. Next to a wide rocky stream, under a proud snowy mountain, in the middle of a fairy-tale forest, a smaller version of me still hurries around, collects her things, and brushes the dirt off them. She'll always be there, trying to right the leaning tent. But she also stands in a stream and holds that steelhead up, decides if he lives or dies. Every time she chooses life and freedom. Always. I like to believe the kiss is not the beast at my center. I like to think the steelhead is there. And that nothing is trapped at the center—it lives there, thrives there.

Tina.

Hi How is my Little girl.
getting Big I Bet. Daddy
Sure misses you. and would
give any thing To give you
a great Big Kiss and Hug
right now. Tina Daddy
Love's you all a whole Bunch
And miss you more and more
every Day. TanyA said she
Love's you To. Daddy is
sending a great Big
Kiss for you all

Kiss me Please

teen starter kit

I WAS SITTING ON THE SCHOOL BUS in an early dream, so they must've started around fourth grade. That was the year Chenowith was overcrowded so they bussed District Nine kids seventeen miles west to Mosier for fourth grade, instead of two miles across town to mix with the District Twelve kids. I was on a bench seat alone but all the other seats were full, two kids each. My head was hanging forward when a tooth fell out of my mouth and landed in my lap. I lifted my hand to feel the empty spot in my gums. I touched another tooth and it was loose, wiggled another and it crumbled between my thumb and pointer finger. My gums were coated in sandy gravel and I started to panic.

Those dreams followed me into high school and beyond but they were most intense in middle school. It always started with a first tooth that came out in one clean, whole piece. Bite into an apple and a tooth gets stuck and comes out, eating cereal a tooth falls into my bowl, sneeze while taking a math test and a tooth lands on the desk. The first one always felt like it could just be a fluke, strange but not too alarming. But as I'd walk through a normal day, more teeth would crumble out. Closing my locker, talking to a boy, giving a speech in class. I'd try to hide the chalky grit in my mouth when talking to people, try to make my lips cover the holes in my gums.

Anything I did to help only made it worse. I'd reach up to check my remaining teeth and cause more teeth to fall apart. Trying to get home to ask for Mom's help, I'd get lost or delayed. I could never make it before waking up. Even after I woke I could feel the grit in my mouth. I'd run to the bathroom to check my teeth in the mirror. Then I'd brush and floss, just to prove I deserved my teeth. Before getting back in bed, I'd kneel on the floor and pray. Prayer felt most effective in the house on Lee Street because those concrete floors were brutal and I was pretty sure prayer worked better if I was physically uncomfortable. I came to associate the feel of my shins crackling against that cold floor with a sense of relief.

We left that house about a month before I finished sixth grade. Mom finally found a way to move us over to District Twelve before Jesse started high school, but just barely. We rented a house on Seventeenth, just above The Dalles Middle School. The owner was a lady from California who only used the house in summer, when she came to windsurf in the Gorge. Mom could afford the rent as long as our landlady had the option to move in with us each summer. So we'd still live in a space that wasn't really ours, but she didn't interfere with us kids at all.

Once, around eighth grade, I woke from the tooth dream in the early morning with an intense urge to run. It was still dark out. I brushed and flossed but instead of praying, I got dressed, put my shoes on, and ran into the dark. Running dissolved my anxiety so it became a habit. When I ran all I thought about was lifting my feet, drawing air, continuing. I didn't plan where I was going or how long I'd run. I just ran until I felt like running back. I slept better once I started running. I never joined cross-country or track; I just ran on my own. But I didn't run on my visits to Loyd. I tried a couple of times but was worried I'd get lost or Loyd's feelings were hurt that I was doing something besides spending time with him. Plus I never knew when I'd get my next shower at Loyd's.

I started to get really self-conscious about my smile. I hated showing my teeth. School picture day was the worst. Photographers were always pushing me to smile with teeth. I could rarely make myself do it and when I did, I'd hate the photo. A month or so after picture day, when the envelopes came back and I brought mine home to Mom, she'd remind me to try to smile next year. She could barely afford to buy the smallest photo package so I felt guilty.

((((((

I'm pretty sure everything that happened in Packwood spun Loyd out into a fresh cycle of frantic substance abuse. Linda and he split up for some time and that didn't help. He ricocheted around his usual territory like a stray bullet and likely left behind some damage as he bounced off people's lives. It was clear we wouldn't see him until he pulled himself together. He called sometimes to explain he was broke and he'd come for us once he found work. Then we started getting cards in the mail, in Linda's handwriting but signed from both of them. I took this to be a sign that things were simmering down. After a while they landed in Camas Valley, a tiny town in the coastal range of southern Oregon.

Uncle Papa and his family were living in Camas Valley. He was working on a small timber outfit between the valley and the coast, and he got Loyd a job on the crew. There wasn't much to Camas Valley. The Chalet Café sat right on Highway 42 next to the gas station, which was also the market and video rental place. One school served all grades, K–12. The nearest big grocery store was about a half hour away in Roseburg.

We went to Camas Valley the summer before I started high school. Loyd and Linda were staying in a small bumper tow trailer at the time, just off Upper Camas Road. It had a bedroom in back, with a door that shut, for Loyd and Linda. The main door opened into a room Loyd built on to the side of the trailer. That's where Jesse and I slept. Our school photos were thumbtacked to the plywood wall. For art, there was a throw blanket from one of those roadside sellers tacked up. Linda called it a tapestry. It was a howling wolf in front of the moon against a dark blue night sky. *Footprints* and *If You Love Something, Set it Free* stuck to the fridge with magnets, both printed over beach scenes and laminated. A macrame plant hanger was over the sink, a spider plant trailing out.

Linda was into coloring those velvet fuzzy posters with pictures of nature and majesty. A doe with two fawns in a forest, a unicorn standing proud on a boulder covered in vines. She'd work on them over several days, blending colors to add depth or shading. If she felt she'd done well, she'd hang one up for a while.

What I remember most about that trailer is its tiny bathroom. It had one of those accordion-style plastic doors, dark brown, made to look like stained wood grain. Seems like it had been misused because we had to be slow and careful when stretching it across the doorway to meet the latch. The latch was a khaki color, which I thought sort of ruined the whole wood effect.

I was self-conscious every time I used that bathroom. I was sure everyone could hear what was happening, as if the bathroom had been designed to amplify and distribute sound through the rest of the trailer. I was sitting on the tiny toilet when I saw my first period had come. Great, I thought, someone's going to hear me opening a crinkly paper wrapper and know.

Mom was pretty sure this might happen. She'd sent some supplies with me when I left, along with this free Teen Starter Kit I'd brought home from school after one of those health classes where they separate the boys from the girls. It had a variety of pads and tampons, an informational pamphlet, and some coupons from Always and Kotex.

My stomach had been hurting all day, just like Mom warned, so I wasn't surprised when I saw my period had started. I was just glad Loyd wasn't home. I stuffed my underwear with toilet paper, ran to grab the teen starter kit from my bag, and ran back. I'd say I yanked the door shut in my hurry but really that's just what I wished I could do. I did try to close it quickly, but that only led to a couple of frustrating misses until I slowed down to guide the little plastic roller on top through the track. Finally the door was shut and latched so I could focus. I mangled my first pad, trying to tear open the package, but still tried to use it. When I stood up it felt wrong so I decided to try another. Jesse tapped on the plastic door.

You gonna be in there all day? I had no idea. Would I? It felt possible, considering the progress I'd made so far. I wasn't sure what the time frame would look like here. I went with an irritated response.

I'm almost done—geez!

Forget it—god! He went outside to pee in the trees. I worried he could tell something was up because he went away without more fighting. After somehow wasting a second pad, I decided I should take my time and read the pamphlet. I was so grateful Mom packed extra pads because the diagrams, instructions, and toxic shock warning in the tampon section of the pamphlet scared me. I was pretty sure I'd never ever use a tampon.

After careful study of the literature, I felt satisfied I'd properly installed the third pad. Though I deeply objected to the use of the word *comfortable* in the pamphlet. It was already clear I'd never feel comfortable for the rest of my life. I gave myself a few extra minutes in the bathroom to settle down. I wanted Mom. I didn't recall her using words like *massacre* or *butcher* when she'd explained what I should expect if my period came while we were apart. But those were the words that best described what I'd just seen so I was a little worried I might have some weird condition that required medical attention.

When I did pull myself together and come out, Linda was waiting. She leaned against the wood paneling of the hallway, her arms crossed in front of her chest and her eyes pulling truth from me like water from a faucet.

Everything OK? Her voice was practical, like she was asking if I'd finished my chores.

Yep.

You need any supplies or are you OK with that? My first instinct was to end this and say I was fine but I wasn't sure that was true. I'd been wondering the same thing. Mom sent me with twelve pads, I used three in ten minutes, and the pamphlet said duration would be five to seven days. I might need more.

I think I need some. I've already used three.

THREE? Jesus. In one trip to the bathroom? My cheeks went red and she backed right off. Clearly I had no idea what I was doing. She looked sorry.

We'll grab some later today, no biggie. She then launched into a tutorial. Proper maxi-pad placement, disposal, duration of use, she just barreled through it like a real trooper. No judgment or excessive eye contact. Just the facts. Love for Linda welled up in my chest.

That evening, I was back in the itty-bitty-potty closet when I heard Linda telling Loyd the big news. I guess the sound transfer worked in both directions because I heard the whole thing. Loyd was headed to the store and she asked him to pick up maxi-pads, giving him a discreet explanation. Loyd's response was not calm.

Shit! Do I need to take her to town to see a doctor?

No Loyd, she's fine. She just needs some pads.

But she's bleeding! There was panic in his voice. After more hushed conversation, Loyd tapped on the plastic door.

OK in there, honey?

Fine, Daddy.

You feeling sick or something? In fact my stomach was upset, but there was no way I was about to muddy these waters.

No, I'm fine. I heard Linda shush him and pull him away. Loyd made like he was whispering, but he was loud.

Well I'm worried! What if she bleeds to death in there? I knew right off it was going to be a long five to seven days. Loyd went to the market/gas station, marched in, and asked the woman at the counter to help him pick out some *lady things* for a girl with her first period. When I picture this, I'm pretty sure the entire town was in the market at that moment.

This was a town where the high school senior class had like six kids in it. The addition of two teenagers in summer did not go unnoticed. Everyone knew who we were and there was only one girl-with-a-first-period Loyd could be buying pads for. We went to the Chalet for dinner the next day and I swear all conversation stopped when we walked in the door. I took off my sweatshirt and tied it around my waist to cover my ass as I followed Jesse to our table. It was the longest walk ever, the only sounds clinking silverware and crushed ice knocking around in those hard plastic diner cups. As we passed, there were more polite *hellos* than felt normal, people calling me *sweetie* and making meaningful eye contact as they greeted us.

While I was still on my period, a group of local boys showed up to invite us swimming. Just in case they hadn't heard, Loyd let them know

I couldn't join them and why. I was just getting ready to step outside the trailer to say hi when I heard Loyd through the screen door.

Oh yeah, they're both here. I bet Jess will wanna go, but not Tina. She's got her first period. You know women don't like to swim with that going on. He said it the way he might whisper about somebody's misfortune, like he was leaning over a fence to tell a neighbor I'd been arrested or was caught cheating on a big test or something.

I wish I could say I'd outgrown my poser phase by then but the truth is, I still hadn't learned the lesson the universe tried to teach me with the whole Cabbage Patch incident. I carried on with similar assholery through middle school and would continue for the first year or so of high school. Begging Mom for Keds when she took me to Volume for ProWings. Esprit bag, Swatch watch, shapeless sweatshirt with the Guess logo across the chest. There was always something I wanted that she couldn't give.

Around this time the spotted owl was pitted against Pacific Northwest loggers in controversy. As timber jobs continued a decades-long decline, environmental regulation became an easy scapegoat. It wasn't unusual to see the bumper stickers around town. *Kill a spotted owl—save a logger* or *I like spotted owls—fried.* I thought the spotted owl was cute and should be saved, when I thought about it at all. Which wasn't much. I was more interested in the Milli Vanilli lip-syncing controversy.

I brought a bunch of *Bop!* and *Teen Beat* magazines with me that summer, along with a box of cassette tapes, most of them singles or blanks I'd recorded from the radio. I had my small boom box and a bunch of batteries since I never knew what to expect from Loyd as far as electricity goes. While Loyd, Linda, and Jesse sat outside in lawn chairs playing cards, or went on walks in the woods, or swimming, I mostly holed up in the room attached to the trailer, listening to music and reading magazines. I'd curl up in my bed nest with the cat for hours. The cat, called *The Kid*, had long black and white fur and the loudest rumbling purr I've ever heard. They named him *The Kid* as a joke, because he was the only child they'd ever share.

Reading teen magazines, I learned all sorts of useless information about teen heartthrobs. I might read about Corey Haim's ideal date or what

Corey Feldman was looking for in a girl. Details like this fueled my romantic imagination about tons of people. Being in love with everyone meant I
didn't have to figure out how to actually be in love with someone. I had a
running fantasy that I'd somehow afford to go to a New Kids on the Block
concert and, through a series of mishaps, I'd meet the band and a couple of
them would fall in love with me. The fantasy plot changed, the love inter-
ests shifting. The only constant was that somehow, I'd end up becoming the
only female member of New Kids on the Block. I was also in love with all
three members of Bell Biv DeVoe but it was hard to create a rich fantasy life
around them because I couldn't find many articles about those guys in *Bop!*
or *Teen Beat.* They mostly seemed to interview white celebrities.

I was sitting on my bed trying to learn the words to the Tiffany song, "I
Saw Him Standing There," by playing it over and over again. Loyd came in,
passing through the room on his way to the fridge to grab a beer. He asked
what I was listening to.

Tiffany.

I don't think I was intentionally short. It was just my dynamic with
Loyd that summer. I'd lost energy for trying to please him. I even tried to
use proper English, or at least what I thought was proper English. It was
natural for me to slip into Loyd's speech patterns when I was with him.
That summer, I tried to resist dropping my g's and saying *ain't.* Most of the
time I forgot. It was habit.

Well, she's singing one of Daddy's old favorites. Did you know this was
a Beatles song?

I don't know why this hit me wrong but my reaction was physical. A
hot line of anger crept up my body and, though I was too old for one of my
childhood fits, I just couldn't let what Loyd said be true. I felt like there was
something at stake, something more important than whose song Tiffany
was signing.

Nuh-uh, it's a Tiffany song.

Well honey, I can hear that's not the Beatles singin' it, I'm just saying
they did when I was young. It didn't help that he'd already annoyed me a
couple of days before by noticing Tiffany's other hit, "I Think We're Alone

Now," was a Tommy James and the Shondells song. He saw I was getting pissed, tried to lighten things up with a little humor.

Hell, them songs played on the radio back when I was smoochin' Mona Pickle. The name of his high school sweetheart had always been a family joke. But I wasn't laughing. I still don't understand why but a frantic panic set in. I was compelled. So I made up a bullshit story.

Duh, the Beatles sang this but only because Tiffany's dad let them. I was careful to seem flippant, like this information was a given. Like everyone knew. Loyd asked a couple of questions, his curiosity sincere. By the end of the conversation, I'd made up an elaborate lie about how Tiffany was an exceptional singer as a toddler, an impression I somehow convinced myself was rooted in truth, and her dad a well-known song-writer. In my lie, Tiffany's dad let other bands use his songs until she was old enough to become a pop star, her obvious destiny. Loyd didn't push or doubt me. He acted like he'd learned something new. I always felt ugly thinking about that story. It exposes not just my bad taste in music, but that I was a lying, snotty asshole. I still don't know if Loyd actually believed me, or if he just didn't know how to step out of our dynamic. I know I didn't.

Jesse decided he wanted to live the school year with Loyd at the end of that summer. My brother was my environment. I'd always lived in relation to him. Jesse kicked my ass many times, but he saved my ass many more. Still, I knew right off there was no way I'd stay with Loyd all school year. We went home to Mom and I watched my brother pack his big, black duffel bag. He threw me a couple of T-shirts he wasn't taking and I wore them all the time, even to school. Before he got in the car to leave, I gave him my school photo with a note on back. *I love you forever. Your sister, Tina.* I felt like it was an important moment but also knew I should keep it cool. I cried a bit when Mom told him to hug me goodbye. It was her big rule, always hug each other goodbye and always make *I love you* the last thing we say to each other. No matter what. My voice cracked a little when I said I loved him. He told me not to be a baby, said he'd see me at Christmas. But he seemed sad, too.

Life without Jesse was scary but I also had new freedom. I walked to school and home alone every day. Missy moved into Jesse's bedroom so I had a room to myself. I'd always been more social than my brother. Now that I had my own room, I didn't mind inviting friends over. It was easier for me to flirt with boys when Jesse wasn't around. I didn't have to worry about him seeing me holding some boy's hand or hearing that I went to a party.

I kissed a couple of boys, both friends I couldn't get excited about even as the kisses happened. After school one day, I found myself walking with a beautiful skater. He just appeared beside me. I was pretty sure I could get excited about him. He had short dark hair, deep brown eyes, and there was something about his jawline that made me want to look at his face all the time. I was worried he'd catch me staring. I knew one of my friends had a crush on him but I kept walking with him anyway. It was exciting, to feel like I was being sneaky.

We didn't talk much at school but we started walking home together most days. I looked forward to it and I think he did, too, because we'd walk really slow. He liked to talk about things I'd never even thought about and found a little scary, like anarchy and The Cure. I took it all to mean he was smarter than me. I was in a Madonna phase and thought the "Like A Prayer" video was sophisticated. I got the idea he thought that was too mainstream. I figured I was, too, so I'd just soak him up for as long as the walking lasted.

We were almost to his house one day and he just stopped walking. It took me a couple of steps to realize it and turn back. He was looking at me in this way that made me want to squirm, like I was in trouble.

Do you want to come in?

I was pretty sure he didn't really like me. I worried about his opinion and knew that I probably wouldn't be able to tell him no, if this headed where I thought it might. Where I hoped it would. I wanted him to want me but I also wanted him to like me, maybe even love me. He watched my face as I worked through it all in my mind.

Don't worry, he said. I just want to show you something.

What?

Remember I told you about that tribe that can shrink human heads?

Yeah ...

I got one. A real one.

I didn't want to see a real shrunken head, but I did want to stay with him. I wanted him to think I was brave. And while the thought of following him down the stairs to his basement bedroom made me nervous, it also thrilled me. My body was already singing.

His bedroom was dark and cool. He pushed play on his tape deck and Depeche Mode came on, "Personal Jesus." He walked over to the dresser, lit incense, and picked up the shrunken head. There was a hole through it, just behind the tiny ears, strung through with a piece of hemp cord, like a necklace. The face looked like leather and it had sparse, wiry hair the color of straw. I was pretty sure it was fake. He asked if I wanted to touch it. I said no. He asked if I wanted to sit. I said sure.

I put my bag down and sat on the edge of his bed. He sat beside me, his thigh touching mine. I focused my eyes on the door. He turned toward me and almost touched his nose to my neck, just behind my ear. Fear was replaced with something else, something entirely new, delivered on a shudder. He exhaled against my neck and it ran all the way down to my toes. I put my hand on his upper arm and it was hard. Skateboarding must've been good exercise because his leg was hard, too, pushed up against me. I wanted to touch all of him. This was all new but it was also familiar, ancient. I knew I could be smashed against his hard body again and again. I thought of the sea, slamming against the rocky cliff back in Clallam Bay, of the driftwood we gathered there, always shaped by the waves. How natural it all felt. I could be shaped, too. I could learn about The Cure and tribes that shrink people's heads. Whatever, I thought, if I get to keep pressing myself against his body, I can be like driftwood.

My mind snagged on that image and I was gone. Standing on the beach in Clallam Bay as Loyd knelt in front of me, holding up a piece of driftwood and asking me to imagine all the things it could be. All the possibility. My body went still next to the beautiful boy. Because I could be hard, too. I could be the one to do the shaping. I didn't say anything to him. I put my hand on his chest and stood up. Then I grabbed my bag and left. I walked up the stairs and into the fall sunshine and I knew it was awkward and prude but I just kept walking.

A year or so later, I'd see a whole display of those shrunken heads in a stall at Portland Saturday Market. It was my first time there. The heads were hanging on pegs, more than I could count, all the same but slightly different, for $10 each. I'd blush with shame, remembering that afternoon. I understood how simple he thought I was, how he knew my world was so small, and how he was right.

That winter, Mom took me and Missy to meet Loyd and Jesse in Packwood at Aunt Rainy's during Christmas break. Auntie and Uncle Papa were coming down from Alaska. Loyd and his siblings hadn't been all together in a few years. Since it was a short trip and the whole family still loved my mom, she was invited, too. We all agreed it sounded fun and we should go but as the weekend approached, I started to feel nervous about it.

We piled into Mom's red 1989 Mazda 323 and took off early in the morning. That Mazda was the first new car my mom ever owned. She had to finance it but she did eventually own it outright, in her own name. I wonder if the thought ever came to her, as we made the drive toward Loyd that Christmas, that this was sort of meaningful. After we fled him all those years ago in a technically stolen car, she was returning on her own terms, in a car he couldn't take from her. She'd eventually give me that car. She let me earn it with good grades and babysitting.

Riding toward Aunt Rainy's that winter, I started to worry over the weekend. I couldn't imagine being with both of my parents on a holiday or really at all. They had forged two completely separate childhoods for me and I was used to that separation. The idea that Missy would be with our dad was also weird. Part of it was just that these two separate casts of characters existed in totally different worlds. But it was also uncomfortable because I was a different person in each of those worlds.

At Mom's, Missy was the baby. We spoiled and picked on her. At Loyd's I was the baby and Loyd seemed to need me to be less capable than I was. I couldn't imagine how to behave with both Loyd and Missy in the same space. Most days I got Missy up and dressed for school. I made her breakfast. I'd given her baths, taken her temperature, and dispensed children's Tylenol. I taught her to read, to add and subtract. I couldn't imagine not being capable for her. But Loyd didn't know me like that and I was so used to slipping into my role with Loyd that I wasn't even aware of it until it came to clash with who I really was. I felt like a faker when I was with Loyd and didn't want Mom or Missy to witness that.

As I rode in the car I don't think I really knew why I was so anxious, just that this didn't feel right. To settle myself I touched each fingertip to my thumb for every painted yellow dash we passed running down the center of the highway, switching hands back and forth as we went. I counted them in tens and got annoyed if Missy did anything to interrupt the cycle because then I'd have to double my speed to catch up, making sure I had acknowledged each dash that was missed.

By the time we pulled into Aunt Rainy's driveway, I'd worried over my fingertips so much that my cuticles were pushed back and raw. Little red half-moons cupped each fingernail and my stomach felt washed out and empty. When they heard our car on the gravel driveway, everyone started to trickle out to greet us. The joy of seeing everybody helped me forget my anxiety, at least for a while.

Mom told lots of our stories at the dinner table that night. The time I was running from Jesse and didn't know Mom had taken the glass out of the screen door to clean it. I thrust my arms forward to push the door but instead flew through it, landing in a huge holly bush, bloody and bruised. The time Jesse was riding his bike down the steep hill next to our house and the front wheel just came right off. A flower delivery lady noticed him lying beside the road so she picked him up and drove him home. And the morning we set the kitchen on fire making toaster waffles before school. My mom worked as secretary in the ER at the hospital and heard our address come across the scanner before I had the chance to call her and tell we were OK. I loved that story because I was the hero. I put the fire out with a bucket before the fire truck even got there. My mom went on telling stories of our years without Loyd and the whole family listened. They were tickled, especially Loyd. Every story testified to our feral ingenuity and made him proud. We might live in *The Big City*, but Loyd didn't have *no soft kids*.

)) ((((

Loyd continued building around the trailer in Camas Valley to create another homestead. When I came back the next summer, he'd added an outdoor kitchen and sitting area. He and Uncle Papa built a structure we called *The Blue Tarp Inn*. The name doesn't really do justice to the Blue Tarp Inn, which was pretty elaborate. I might even call it fancy, in the context of Loyd's life. The Blue Tarp Inn was yurt-shaped, with a blue tarp roof. It had a huge, polished wood-slab bar and barstools made of wide tree trunks that were topped with soft cushions Loyd made himself with rich blue velvet and shiny gold upholstery tacks. Loyd used wood he harvested as much as possible to create a rustic look. *Who needs to go to the tavern when you got your own?*

We went to the Douglas County fair in Roseburg and Loyd made us get those old-timey western photos taken. He'd done similar photos with Aunt Rainy and Uncle Papa a couple of years back and *had a real hoot*. Engineering the photos was serious business for Loyd, deciding on the props, clothing, and positioning. He did one with Jesse and one with me. In Jesse's, they're both dressed as outlaws and holding guns. In mine, I'm dressed like a saloon prostitute with a feather boa, wide-brimmed hat, and garter showing on my thigh. My right hand is on my hip and my left rests on Loyd's shoulder, my fingers wrapped around the neck of an Old Grand-Dad 80 proof Kentucky straight bourbon bottle. Loyd is sitting, wearing a fringed fur-trapper jacket with two wide bandoliers full of shells coming down both shoulders to cross at his lower chest, a shotgun resting across his lap. He's wearing his own hat and it fits right in.

Loyd hung the Wild West photos in the Blue Tarp Inn. Tacked up next to each other, staggered so Jesse's was just a bit higher than mine, on the unfinished cedar plank wall behind the bar. They fit the place in their fake parchment paper folders, printed to look like old frames. Besides the dartboard, these were the only decorations in the Blue Tarp Inn.

Camas Valley summer revolved around the local swimming holes. We'd go to the Middle Fork Coquille River or one of the small ponds in the area. One day, some boys came to invite me and Jesse swimming. I ran inside to put my swimsuit on and get ready.

Mom and I shared a collection of second-hand swimsuits and she'd helped me pick a good one to pack to Camas because I was worried about it. I usually wore a bikini at home but didn't want to do that around Loyd. We decided on a one-piece with wide pink and white stripes, full butt coverage, and minimal cleavage. I pulled it up, put my long basketball shorts and Trailblazers T-shirt back over it, and went out to jump in the car. Loyd was working in the garden but he stopped and stood at attention as I squeezed in behind the folded front seat to press myself into the back between two boys. Jesse got in front. Loyd's head went up like he was sniffing something on the breeze. He walked over to lean down at Jesse's window and say goodbye, said he was getting awful hot and might just join us in a bit.

Jesse and I gave each other space at the river, settled into separate little groups. He didn't seem to like it much, that some of the boys were hanging around with me. But he didn't say anything. I splashed around, cussing and bragging about the sort of trouble we got up to in The Dalles. I made snarky jokes at the boys, insulting their intelligence, dared them to pursue me, had no idea what I'd do if they did. I wasn't really good at flirting, but I liked to try.

When Loyd and Linda pulled up, I'd taken off my shorts and T-shirt. I stood in my swimsuit, waist deep in the water with three boys in my circle. Loyd looked at me so hard I could feel it. It was a look that told me I had reason to feel ashamed. Linda set out a blanket on shore, opened a beer, and lit a cigarette. Loyd set down the ice chest, making more noise than necessary, yanked his shirt off, and flung it down behind him as he made his way to the water in his cutoff jean shorts with frayed strings hanging down his thighs. He dove in and swam straight to me.

When he surfaced, he made sure to get us all wet. He exaggerated a comic tone, trying to cover up the snarl in his voice, as he asked, you kids gonna swim or just stand around yapping? He shook off on us, poked fun at the boys. They were strutting before Loyd showed up but now they were all calm and respectful. Loyd finally looked at me. Up and down.

I think you need something to eat, he said. He grabbed my wrist and tugged me to the shore. I plopped onto the blanket and he threw a towel at me. I understood I should cover up. He didn't explain and I stayed on that blanket next to Linda until everyone else was done swimming and it was time to go.

I went to bed early that night and faked sleep just to avoid Loyd. I heard Linda try to talk to him at the back of the trailer.

It's a very modest suit, Loyd. I'm not sure why it bothers you so much. Other girls are wearing bikinis. She can't help it if boys look.

It bothers me because she looks like a whore in that goddamned swimsuit! It was all I ever heard him say on the topic. I swam the rest of that summer in shorts, a sports bra, and a tank top. But I was glad I heard what Linda said.

I have a photo of Linda taken at the place with the Blue Tarp Inn. It's my only photo of her. I mean, there are others but she's usually in the background or in a group. Most of the time Linda took the pictures. So this is the only photo I have that is just Linda—she's the subject.

She's standing at the outdoor kitchen and the garden is behind her. It must be late summer because the marigolds are bursting bright orange and the cosmos are tall, hot pink, and popping out of the background to surround her like the holy mother. Tassels are already forming at the tops of the corn stalks and the countertop is brimming with harvest. Her hair is pulled up in the messy bun of a woman who has long given up on her physical appearance. Her hair is all whitish-gray. I don't know her age. I think she was a little older than Loyd so she was likely in her late forties or early fifties, but she looks older.

I can tell she's making Loyd's favorite *fried taters*. She's standing at the cutting board, paring knife in her right hand and half a potato in her left. The cutting board is already piled with sliced potatoes. She's clearly stopped mid-slice to turn toward the camera and humor Loyd with a forced smile. Like always, she shares only half her face, half her smile. Even then, her smile is protected, hiding her bad teeth. I can hear the quick dry laugh of exasperation that came as she turned toward him. I know it must be Loyd behind the camera because she only looked at Loyd the way she's looking.

Linda took tons of photos during our Camas Valley summers. I can tell she was trying to be artistic. I found a photo of me that looks like she must have crouched down behind some tall grasses to take the picture. The green blades are in the foreground and I'm walking beside shallow water, a long T-shirt over my swimsuit, watching my step as I walk on bare feet over a rocky shore. I didn't know she was taking the picture and I was surprised when I found it because I thought she only ever took pictures with Loyd in them.

She wrote dates on most of the photos from Camas, her flowing cursive recording our time together. I find it remarkable she felt the urge to take and date so many photos. It's completely out of pattern with all our years together. I wonder if Linda understood these were our last couple of summers together. Or maybe she was just reacting to the obvious distance opened up between Loyd and me. Maybe she was trying to give him something he could keep, since I was clearly slipping away.

Once, Linda asked me to take a picture of her and Loyd. I remember it because she never wanted her picture taken. I have this photo in my hands now. She's sitting in a metal lawn chair and he's standing behind her. It's one of those chairs left over from the fifties. The seat and back are powdery teal blue, the tubular arms and legs white. Loyd's hands are on the arms of the chair and he's leaning down so his chin almost rests on the top of Linda's head. His hat looked like the one Indiana Jones wore and had a small hole worn in the front peak, from where Loyd would grab it with his thumb and pointer finger to lift it in greeting. He wore a hat pretty much all the time, ever since a bald spot started in his late twenties. There's no date on the back of that photo of Linda with Loyd. Instead she wrote, *I will always love you, Loyd.* And that turned out to be true.

high five

LOYD WAS NEVER FAMILIAR to me the way Mom was. I never crawled into his bed when I was afraid or woke him in the night to ask questions that couldn't wait until morning, questions about God and the universe. Like the time I woke with a sudden and desperate need to know where we go after we die. I tiptoed into Mom's room. She was clearly asleep but I touched her shoulder anyway.

Mom, are you asleep? Nothing.

Mom, can I sleep with you? Nothing. I climbed in. I tried to go to sleep, be comforted by her warm body next to me, her soft snore like a song. But the need to know wouldn't go away.

Mom? Pause. Mom? Pause. Mom?

What? It wasn't her patient voice.

Where do we go when we die?

Long exhale but no answer.

Like, I know we don't have bodies anymore, but where do we GO?

I don't know, Tina. Go to sleep.

Can we still see? Can we even see after we die?

Honey, I have to work in a few hours. It's probably just dark. Like nighttime. Or like when your eyes are closed or you're asleep.

I pushed my lips together. I wanted to be a kid who could just roll over and go to sleep. I counted my fingers again and again, touching each fingernail under the thumb and flicking upward, evenly on both hands in sync, while pressing my wrists against my chest. When I'd done all four fingers, I'd flick the thumb under the pointer finger, finishing up the sequence. Repeat. Repeat. Still, I couldn't fall asleep.

Are there stars? If it's like nighttime? Can we still see the stars?

Tina, go to sleep or go back to your own bed. I knew she'd had enough so I pretended to fall asleep while the question spun out in my head, creating a whole constellation of new stars flaming to life in a dark galaxy. This happened a lot. I'd float around in all that unknowing and worry, not sure if I'd ever land on something solid, until I drifted off or morning came.

One thing I knew. My mom belonged to me. I never felt ownership of Loyd. So he was less necessary but also, until Packwood, more adored. He was novel, rare, something often lost to me. Mom was constant, imperfect but going nowhere without me. And what do we take for granted as much as our most familiar things? We give the least care to those worn out with comforting us. Now I recognize that my mom's kind of love was a tattered constant and I should've taken better care of her.

《 《 《

The Dalles is a threshold, gateway between the pristine green of western Oregon and the dry eastern desert that runs on to meet Idaho. It's always been a place of meeting and of passing through. The mighty river carried and fed people long before it was called *Columbia*, before white people pushed their way West. The Wishram and the Wasco, the Yakama and the Chinook, the Klickitat and the Warm Springs. Before the falls were swallowed, snowmelt flooded over the basalt cliffs in spring, filling the channels and choppy water with salmon. People came from as far as the Great Plains to fish and trade. Later, the Columbia carried fur traders, Lewis and Clark, westward wagons, barges loaded with goods.

Today, Interstate 84, Highway 30, and Highway 97 all meet at The Dalles, still a place of intersection. The Dalles Bridge crosses over to Washington in front of the dam. Semitrucks carry freight in all directions. Migrating farm workers travel through each spring to gather cherries, apples, pears, and grapes. Boats sit in the river fishing or move through the locks, lifted or lowered depending on their destination. Trains carry gas and oil along the riverbank. Meth, heroin, and other opioids flow through in the trunks of cars, polluting the people along the way.

For me, being a teenager in The Dalles in the nineties was also like standing on a threshold. So much about that time and place felt like transition, the space between destinations. We'd watched the fall of the Berlin Wall and knew it meant something, even if we weren't sure what. We gathered in the living rooms of kids who had cable, dancing along with Club MTV, and Downtown Julie Brown felt like proof that we lived in a free world where everyone had a fair shot.

Oregon was the progressive leader of the nation when it came to gay rights. Even in The Dalles most folks opposed Measure 9, legislation crafted by the Oregon Citizen's Alliance to strip gay people of their civil liberties. My boyfriend and I stumbled into an opposition march in Portland one day and joined in, screaming and feeling strong. *We're here, we're queer, get used to it!* Still, the word *gay* was thrown around openly as an insult in the school hallways and none of my classmates would come out until long after we graduated and left. We'd grown up in the shadow of Ryan White. It was a national news story, a child ousted from school, harassed, and threatened because he'd been infected with HIV by a medical procedure. Ryan White introduced many of us to the idea of injustice, and gave us our first urge to fight on the behalf of a stranger. With the simple logic of children, we'd come to question the idea that a disease could be punishment for sin. It followed that we'd oppose the idea of loving somebody as sin. Still, we internalized the fear at the center of Ryan White's story. People would hate you and hurt you for being gay, or even associated with gayness.

Like people in most small towns, we believed race wasn't an issue anymore. The United Colors of Benetton taught us that all different kinds of people could hug and kiss and wear fashionable clothes together. Rodney King showed us otherwise. Most kids at The Dalles High School would say they didn't see color, a popular claim back then. It's easy not to see color when there isn't much color to see. Oregon is a very white state, even now. While those same kids probably didn't use racial slurs, I'm pretty sure we all sat quiet in conversations while the words *spic* and *beaner* flew around. Though there were kids of color in my class, there's a way they were asked to be invisible. So were the poor kids. We were all expected to act as if we had equal access to the Benetton dream. It was easier for me because I was white. I sat there plenty of times while kids talked shit about *trailer trash* and *welfare moms,* as if I'd never eaten a meal bought with food stamps, lived in a trailer, or slept at somebody's house because we didn't have one of our own. I used the term *white trash* so nobody would figure out that's what I was.

In my days at The Dalles High School, our mascot was the Indians and each year at homecoming we competed for the Tomahawk award. There's a way white people convince one another that messing around in a stereotype of somebody else's culture is a compliment. I thought noth- ing of painting stripes on my face like the rest of the girls when we took the field to play football in a gender-reversed homecoming tradition. When I watched a white upperclassman holding the coveted Tomahawk trophy while dancing to a drumbeat and wearing a feather headdress on the gym floor during the homecoming assembly, I want to say I knew it was wrong. In reality my only reaction was to develop another unre- quited crush.

I don't know for sure when I started drinking. By the end of ninth grade, I usually had at least ten Natty Lights tucked away in my closet at any given time. Mom's pain really started to catch up with her by then. Her medicine appeared in twenty-four-packs, had a permanent space in the bottom right corner of the fridge. If I waited until late in the evening, I could take one and add it to my stash without notice.

I had plenty of access to other alcohol. Me and my friends saved Snap- ple bottles, with wide mouths and screw on lids, so we could pour in an inch or two from any liquor our parents had around the house. When we had money, it was easy to find someone to buy for us. Friends of my older cousins, or drunks we'd find sitting around in front of Safeway. When I'd hang out with the farm kids, we'd use their CB radios to find truckers passing through and willing to meet at Albertson's to buy us Mad Dog 20/20. It was easier if a girl did the talking.

My locker partner lived near the high school and sometimes I left early to go to her house before first period. One morning, I watched as she mixed small pours from her mom's fancy liquor cabinet into an empty paper Pepsi cup. I didn't object. Not when she carried it to school or when she invited others to come have a drink at our locker. I was always up for a good time.

I was in English, the period right after lunch, when Mr. Bull came to get me out of class. I knew they'd probably come for me at some point that day, was a little surprised it took them so long. Still, English was my favorite class and I was ashamed to be called out like that. Mr. Bull only ever came for the trashy kids.

I walked a couple of steps behind him down the silent hall. He was an administrator and a sports guy so I'd never interacted with him before. He was tall, broad shoulders stretching a cotton polo shirt across his back. He didn't explain why he'd come for me or even speak at all. But I knew I was in hot shit.

I was ready to face whatever punishment, but when they sat me down and told me to call my mom, I about lost it. The principal pushed his rotary phone toward me across his desk. I met his eye and asked right away if I could take extra punishment instead of calling my mom at work. I just couldn't face that I was adding something like this to her shoulders. I got good grades, took my sister places when Mom needed me to. I wanted to be a kid who made her worry less, not more. He said no so I called the hospital and asked for her in the polite tone she'd taught me. I waited, freezing cold, for her to come. When she walked into the school, she had a look on her face I'd never seen before.

I was suspended and had to go to counseling. Group once a week and one-on-one meetings with the drug and alcohol counselor. I really liked her. She had short salt-and-pepper hair, wore glasses, and made no effort to look pretty. She told me that anything I said in our private meetings, except for current abuse or neglect, stayed between us. So I told the truth. I didn't

offer anything, but I answered her honestly, and she had good questions. I
didn't tell her about Packwood or any specific incident that her direct questions didn't force out. But by the end of our first meeting, she informed
me that my dad was an addict. She sent me to a few Al-Anon meetings
and I learned a lot, even if I didn't choose to go anymore once I'd met the
requirements of my punishment.

I'd never been to a counselor before, never had somebody stand outside my life and analyze what they saw. But once I picked up the idea, I
couldn't stop. Suddenly, all the lessons Loyd taught, all the times he didn't
show up, all the fights and drama, made a new kind of sense. And it all fed
the anger I'd been growing in my belly since Packwood.

I didn't yet know that I'd already spent my last summer visit with Loyd.
I didn't see how the swimsuit was the beginning, a signal that I was no
longer able to hide my maturity. And I don't just mean my changing body.
Loyd had always poked fun at my *book smarts* and I was now old enough
to recognize that as insecurity. School was the first place I ever heard of
Shakespeare, Jane Austen, Mary Shelley. Before tenth-grade English, I
thought Frankenstein was just the guy from *The Munsters* and the closest
I'd come to *Henry IV* was watching *My Own Private Idaho*, not for intellec-
tual stimulation, just for Keanu Reeves. But I started to seek out books like
this, even when the reading wasn't required. I volunteered, shelving books
at the public library. I was encouraged to skip ahead a year in English. It
made me feel legitimate somehow, being set apart like that. I was filling my
story with new characters and the more I learned, the more space there was
between Loyd and me.

That winter, Jesse wanted to go see Loyd during break. I told him I
wasn't sure I wanted to go. Mom took me aside and said I should. My life
was filling up. Friends, babysitting in summer, my part-time job as a file
clerk at the hospital. Mom thought, with Jesse graduating and enlisting
in the Coast Guard, I might not go see Loyd in the summer anymore so
maybe this trip was a good idea. Jesse had his own car, a Ford EXP he'd
bought from my aunt Connie with $400 he earned bagging groceries at
Albertson's. It had no backseat but he was always making me ride in back

anyway, so his buddy Phil could ride up front. We piled into the EXP and drove to meet Loyd at Aunt Rainy's for a few days during Christmas break.

Uncle Papa and his family were coming down again so I got pretty excited about the trip. When everyone heard us pull up, they all rushed out and my anger cracked apart when Loyd crushed me in his arms. He always squeezed just a little too hard and I came to need that sort of pressure to feel really loved. I pulled away from him and hugged Uncle Papa and Aunt Rainy. Each of them had that same gleam of tearful love in their eyes.

Loyd and his siblings were crazy close. They loved each other like I've never seen. They could talk without saying hardly anything and they only ever called each other *Bro* or *Sis*. It was a love that the rest of us accepted as impenetrable. Loyd always tried to live someplace close to either Uncle Papa or Aunt Rainy. They created the boundaries of his territory.

I remember once we were in Camas Valley and putting together a barbeque with Uncle Papa's family. While Linda prepared food, Loyd and Uncle Papa ran to the market for beer. After an hour they weren't back so we thought maybe they'd decided to go all the way to Winston or Roseburg. Another hour passed and we were pretty sure they'd stopped at the bar or something. Finally we ate without them, said goodbye, and went our separate ways. Loyd was still gone at bedtime. Turns out, they'd been talking on the way to the store and realized they both had a hurt to see *Sis*. They stopped at the store, got the beer, but then kept on driving down the highway. Six hours later Aunt Rainy heard the unmistakable racket of her two *Bros* laughing and hollering as they stumbled up onto her porch. *Open up Sis, we brought beer!*

Our visit to Aunt Rainy's that Christmas break started out great. Loyd was proud to have us there with his family and he was mellow, no sign of the wolf. We'd eat a big meal each night, then the kids would go into the family room to watch TV and play darts while the adults played cards. Whenever Loyd got together with his siblings, they played a game they called *High Five*. Someone in the family had invented High Five, farther back than anyone could remember. Only adults were taught to play and we'd be reminded of that every time we asked to join. I never did learn to play High Five.

After dinner we'd clear the table, do the dishes, and the adults would set the table with ashtrays, cans of beer, and bowls of chips to start playing their hours-long game of High Five. All us kids headed out to the TV room and sprawled out on the couch and floor. This was the dynamic when we were all together, kids to be seen and not heard, but I always had the sense it was hard on Loyd. When he was with us, he liked to be with us. Aunt Rainy and Uncle Papa had their kids all the time so it was different for them.

On the last night of that visit, Loyd kept popping out to the family room when he took a break from cards. He'd use the bathroom out there, instead of the one that was closer to the card game, just to check in on us. When he passed through, he'd joke at Jesse, lean down to kiss the top of my head or just touch my shoulder as he passed. Jesse was on the couch with my cousins, Danny and Nate. Loyd walked by them, tilted his hip to a ridiculous angle, aimed, paused, then ran off, throwing his head back to holler.

SBD!

He giggled as the boys jumped up, waving their hands in front of their faces. Then they started to wrestle, trying to force each other toward the imagined noxious cloud of smell Loyd left. For Loyd, the silent-but-deadly-and-run trick never got old.

Nate, who was just a little younger than Jesse, flipped through the channels until he landed on *Porky's*. At one point, Loyd passed through the room and noticed what we were watching. I'm not sure he'd even know what *Porky's* was, but he caught it at a racy moment. He told Nate to change the channel. Jesse said we'd seen it before, and reminded Loyd he was just days away from turning eighteen.

That don't mean you all need to see this shit.

Why? Nate asked.

Because I said so. This ain't the kind of stuff you kids need to be watching.

Why not? Nate asked again.

There's little girls here, that's why not. Do I gotta change it for you?

Nate flipped the channel with a little attitude and Loyd left. As soon as he was gone, Nate changed it back. I kind of hated *Porky's*. I could never understand what was so funny. But I wasn't about to say anything. When we heard Loyd heading our way again, Nate changed the channel. But Loyd could tell something was up, noticed the odd silence between us and that it was about him. He gave me a peck on the top of my head, ruffled Jesse's hair. He shot Nate a nasty look. It felt like picking teams in gym class. Loyd was claiming us. Nate had been sneaking beers and was feeling defiant. I got the feeling we were in for some shit.

Each time Loyd came out, Nate changed the channel and we'd pass around knowing glances like we were playing telephone. He started pushing his luck, waiting a beat longer before changing the channel, exhaling a quiet smirk through his nose as Loyd passed. It actually reminded me of Loyd, holding bottle rockets too long, pushing things as close as possible to the edge. Nate was toying with Loyd. What he didn't know is that he was also forcing us to choose. Be loyal to our dad or be cool, one of the kids.

I don't think Nate had any idea about the distorted sense of loyalty we were always trying to balance with our parents. It matters a whole lot when your parents split. Our time with Loyd, every interaction, was shaped by the humiliation of our mom leaving him. It was the great failure of Loyd's life and Jesse and I were always making up for it. But Nate didn't know that. He was just screwing around. And Nate was seventeen, still a kid. Loyd should be the adult here. Instead, he started to see his nephew as a rival. I saw the future coming at us, could hear the old song in my head, knew every beat, how it would build and climax. I was so tired of that song.

When I'd gone to my required Al-Anon meetings, I always got caught up in the stories other kids would tell. I shared as little as possible in those meetings. But the empathy and sense of injustice I felt for others when they shared was so strong. More than once, I'd walked another kid to the counselor's office at school because I knew they needed help they weren't getting from the world. Something about that experience combined with the analytic skills I'd picked up in my private counseling sessions, and I started to look at my own stories. I even started talking with Mom about it a little. I was always careful not to share anything that would add to her burden, but our talks gave solid form to many shapeless memories I carried.

One gift Loyd gave me is a habit for distancing myself from my relationships. Maybe it's just a side effect of constantly having my relationship with my dad put on pause. Standing outside and looking into my life had become habit. I know it can be frustrating to the people I love, the way I retreat to analyze. But it's a hard-earned skill. By the time we came to Aunt Rainy's that winter, I'd really been thinking about my dad and our history. I'd even been writing about it and those words were with me that night. All of this is just to say that I was ready to unleash on Loyd, something I'd never felt before.

When we'd first arrived at Aunt Rainy's, I'd been disarmed by Loyd's warmth and the joy of being reunited with the whole family. As the tension grew between him and Nate, my anger returned. Here we were in Packwood again, place of my greatest shame. That shame was buried, even from me, at the time. Still, though I couldn't call it to mind and define it, it was there. The kiss was a frozen thing, solid, resting in my gut. It sat at the bottom of my esophagus, always threatening to jump up my throat and out my mouth. An eruption I had no time for, a wave I kept running from, always running. Sometimes I wonder, who would I be if I didn't have that kiss to run from?

Loyd started to visit the TV room more frequently. He'd accepted Nate's invitation to dance. I recognized the way his expression deepened each time, the way he avoided Nate until he didn't, until the visits were all about Nate. Both of their voices changed when they spoke to each other. It was like a complicated opera with harmonies and precise blocking, predictable patterns and intimacy between performers. As a watcher, I'd always floated on those conventions and let them sweep me up in their beauty and drama. I couldn't help but be enthralled.

Except not this time. Now all the seams were obvious, the clockwork exposed. I felt tired, a sudden and heavy sleepiness. I thought about escaping. I knew I could go to the other room, go to bed, wake in the morning and hear the silence surrounding what happened. Sleep and not know. Let it be another truth I'd never fully learn. Instead I decided to stay awake and witness one more time. It was a deliberate choice. I walked to the bathroom attached to the TV room.

I closed the door and started talking to myself, quietly, lips moving. This is something I did as a child when Loyd was hitting. Something I still do when I need to coach myself before a confrontation. Practice what I'd say if I found the courage to stand up. I thought I was in the rare position to get through to Loyd. I believed I was precious to him in a way that could clear his fog of anger. I was like that guy who went to live with the bears in Alaska and thought they wouldn't kill him because he understood them, had gained their trust. Or the lady who had her face ripped off by her pet chimpanzee. I was foolish when it came to the truth of Loyd's nature. He was a man but the wolf was a wild animal.

From the bathroom, I listened to Loyd and Nate continue their slow escalation and coached myself to intervene. I thought about the years I'd spent watching Loyd, the countless times I'd sat in this same sort of simmering tension. Waiting with anxiety. Will it blow up this time, or will Loyd laugh and walk away? Either option kept me trailing behind, trying to keep my head up in the wake of his urges. Once it was clear he wouldn't walk away, there was always the simple fight or flight response. The power starting in my middle and pushing through my body, straight up and down. I stood tall and waited for instinct, which felt infallible in those moments, to animate me. As a child, that feeling in my body sent me hiding or running away. Sometimes crawling into bed to fake sleep, my back facing the sounds of Linda trying to be quiet.

This time, instinct made me feel strong. I was done. I opened the door so I could keep an eye on things. I watched for the moment of transition like a midwife timing contractions, waiting for birth. I washed my face. Closed the door to change into my sweatpants. Opened the door again to monitor. Loyd moved closer to the couch where Nate was stretched out with his smartass crooked grin. I pulled my toothbrush from its plastic sandwich bag, was slow to apply toothpaste, more precise than usual because the song had started and everything was caught in its rhythm now. Timing is important.

I was brushing my teeth to the beat when Nate came up to a sitting position. They were stepping toward the transition, but carefully. They both wanted it enough to avoid drawing the attention of the adults in the other room. Sometimes, I wonder that I didn't have the sense to walk out to the card game and get help. Maybe I wanted it too, my chance to jump into the fray. I bent to the sink to rinse my mouth with water. In the mirror I saw Nate stand to face Loyd. Nate's chest was wider and he was taller. I ran my toothbrush under the faucet and tapped it one, two, three times on the side of the sink. Like a magic tone my tap, tap, tap broke the filmy surface of calm and invited in the wolf. The song swelled toward its peak, Loyd pushing his chest into Nate's. I looked at myself one more time, my hands on either side of the sink. Young face, old eyes. Nate put both his big palms on Loyd's chest and gave a little shove.

I turned from the mirror and walked into the family room. Jesse and I shared a knowing look. I thought we silently agreed that I'd step in, that our siblinghood had granted us a sort of ESP. We weren't children anymore and it was time to do something about this.

Loyd took a swing. It was a strike I'd seen before, a quick and short right-hand pop from up close, meant to start things off and win the first point. But Nate was fast and dodged it so Loyd just grazed his cheek. Nate returned and landed a fist on Loyd's chin. Again, I was struck by the way Loyd seemed to enjoy being hit, the force absorbing into his body and giving him more fight. I rushed them just as Loyd's elbow wound back for another punch, this one designed for greater impact. Jesse got there first.

Apparently our sibling telepathy was just another thing I'd always imagined. Before I could put myself between Loyd and Nate, my bother was there. Jesse shoved Nate away and Loyd's punch busted my brother's lip. Bright red blossomed out of Jesse's mouth. It was reluctant to emerge at first, a slow bubble peeking out as we all watched. But then it came with more confidence and sang out as only blood can. My brother's blood called me to a sort of attention I have rarely known. Jesse's pink-cheeked face and his obvious injury startled Loyd. My brother looked like a man, but also like the boy he once was. When his head got sweaty, that front piece of hair would still rise to stand up. It did so now. Everything stood at attention. I stepped in front of Loyd.

Stop! Just fucking stop! My voice was loud enough to carry into the other room.

At school, I cussed a lot. Cussing was like a competitive sport for me, made me feel like a badass, and I excelled. But I'd never used the f-word, or any other expletive, in front of my dad. Now I used that word and many more he didn't expect. This time, I guess I transformed in front of Loyd, instead of the other way around. My diction changed instantly because I was using counselor speak, mixed with angry foul language, to explain to Loyd all the ways he damaged us. I was articulate in a way he'd never seen, a person he'd never really met. He froze as I shamed him in front of every-one, including his brother and sister, who'd both rushed in to see what the hell was going on. I stood facing Loyd and was so focused on him that I didn't notice the signals Jesse sent, letting me know it was over and I should shut up.

Looking back, it's no surprise Jesse beat me to the fight. I'd so often run away when he stayed and witnessed. He knew the dance better than I did. He was better prepared to step in. But he was also the family peacemaker, always smoothing things over. Jesse's goodness was something everyone agreed on. And that made the blood on his face a greater violation. The smile I'd known the longest and best was my brother's. I learned to talk from watching his lips. His mouth made the words that led me to safety more times than I could remember. And Loyd broke his lip like it was noth-ing, like Jesse was another *nagging woman* or drunk in a bar.

We all begin as tubes. When we're formed, I mean, when cells start to multiply and make us, the first shape is a tube. One end becomes a mouth. I'm sure it's obvious what the other end becomes. Everything else is built up around this first structure, the line that runs through our core. I only bring it up because I always felt aware of my core, when I was with the wolf. Each time I stood like that, feeling the power run through the center of my body as I waited for the worst to happen, each time the line grew and I stood taller. Through the years, this space filled up with everything I never said to Loyd. All I'd witnessed but couldn't express was locked up in the tunnel at my center. Swimming lessons and chocolate pudding, Mom's bruises and Linda's cries, Uncle Tom and CC. The kiss. All of it was there, trapped.

In the Paul Bunyan stories from my childhood, there was a winter so cold that words coming out of a logger's mouth would freeze before anyone could hear them. Paul's camp was silent all winter, no matter what the lumberjacks tried to say. There was nothing for it but to live in silence until the spring came. When the world started to thaw, the racket was unbearable. All those frozen words suddenly bursting into sound.

I opened my mouth and broke Loyd's heart. I told him this wasn't normal, that he was hitting Jesse and Nate. Kids. I asked him, Is this what a man does? Is this what a father does? I told him other kids didn't have to watch their dad fight all the time. Other kids had dads that took them to school, helped with homework. I said I was sick of it and never wanted to see or hear him hit anyone again, so if he wanted to see me, he'd have to do better. I thought it would feel amazing but I was uncomfortable the whole time. I felt cold and shaky, like when you're waiting for surgery, or for a cop to call in your driver's license. I had to force myself to stay on the script in my head and push past the trembling in my voice.

Loyd stayed quiet, just looked at me with shining eyes. When I finished he didn't argue or respond. Uncle Papa led him away for a smoke while Aunt Rainy talked with the boys, rubbed Jesse's back. Moments before, I really thought Loyd would hear me, that somehow I'd start some change in him. And maybe it would've worked if I hadn't said those things in front of his siblings. But all I'd done is humiliate him. I was the villain in that room. Everyone knew we couldn't expect much else from Loyd. I felt like I'd punched a toddler or something.

Loyd didn't speak to me that night or the next morning, as we got ready to head home. We gathered in the driveway, Jesse's car packed up and ready to go. Loyd didn't reach for me or say anything. I hugged him anyway, but it was quick and stiff. I said I loved him. It was Mom's most important rule, always say *I love you*, always hug goodbye, no matter what. He was playful with Jesse, said he'd see him in summer. He didn't mention summer to me.

When we got home and Mom asked how it went, I told her the truth for once. There was no hiding Jesse's busted lip, but it was more than that. Something had broken for me, too. She promised me that Loyd loved me as much as ever. She said he just didn't know how to work out problems and it wasn't a child's job to teach him. Then she told me my own story, a story I couldn't really see because I was inside it. It was about a girl who was always trying to be what her dad wanted, a girl who grew too smart to keep pretending, and about a man who never learned the right way to love people. The moral was that the girl didn't get to have a father who took care of her. That just wasn't part of her story. Mom apologized for that, said it was her fault.

My mom always loved me in a way that taught me I could never be lower than she was. She didn't just lift me up and push me forward, she put herself down. She'd tell me she messed it all up, kids should be raised by two parents, not just one. People should go to college and make a decent living before having children. I felt like I had a responsibility to do better, but like I was supposed to leave her behind in the process. In some ways, this talk saved me. In other ways, it made me harsh. I was always delivering some verdict against my parents. Now, it just makes me sad. Truth is, I've never worked as hard as Mom at anything. Working, raising my children, keeping them fed and clothed, housed and healthy, has all been easier for me because I have a partner, health insurance, and stable income.

Today, my mom still buries herself beneath us. She takes the blame for all our failures but won't give herself credit for any of our accomplishments. When we stumble, she thinks it's something she did or a lack of mothering. She made her body a bridge for us and I walked over that bridge to get out of poverty. She acts like I did it all alone. I wish I could make her see herself with the same grace she's always given me.

When Jesse graduated high school, Loyd and Linda came to the ceremony. They drove the six hours from Camas in their maroon Ford Pinto.

Loyd didn't like driving out of town since he never renewed his tags and his driver's license was expired. There's also a good chance there was a warrant or two out there for him, so you know Jesse's graduation meant a lot to him. It was their second Pinto. Jesse had wrapped the blue one around a tree the year he lived in Camas Valley. Loyd didn't have insurance, health or auto, but it's not like he would've filed a claim on that Pinto anyway since Jesse didn't have a license yet when it happened.

Loyd showed up the morning of Jesse's graduation with a garbage bag full of cheap stuffed animals. Missy loved Loyd. She always laughed at his fart jokes and clowning around. She was still a little kid and gave him the sort of attention I was no longer capable of. I was jealous that the gift was for Missy. I'd been nervous to see Loyd again. He greeted me with a hug, but it felt cool. When Missy opened the bag Loyd brought and started pulling out those stuffed animals, I didn't want them or anything. They were the stiff, unattractive kind, like you win at carnivals. I just didn't like that Loyd brought them for her and not me. But then he jabbed me with his elbow like I was in on a joke and asked if I remembered the claw machine at the Chalet. Apparently, Loyd had walked in a couple weeks before and noticed they'd put a crisp hundred-dollar bill in the damn thing. It was attached, by paper clip, to a neon orange bear. Loyd figured that *hunerd bucks* would make a fine graduation gift for Jesse.

Tina Marie, I'll be goddamned if I wasn't gonna get that cash, Loyd said. Figured I'd spend up to seventy-five bucks trying. Well kids, I spent eighty and never got that money but I got damn-near, I'm telling you. And now I got me a shit-ton of these little critters and I figured the little squirt might want 'em. Something about the story, the way he was making fun of himself and inviting me into that, broke the silence between us. It might just seem like a silly story, but I understood it was a peace offering.

After graduation we came back to the house and I helped Mom make tacos for everyone. Loyd acted all impressed that I could brown ground beef and throw in a packet of taco seasoning. We sat around visiting, listening to the oldies and playing Yahtzee, the adults smoking cigarettes and drinking beer. Jesse didn't go to the all-night party with his classmates. He never felt the drive to join those things like I did. I can still see Jesse across the living room, his face looking so young, a haze of smoke between us. "These Boots are Made for Walking" playing on the radio, Mom swaying because she could never resist that song. Loyd's eyes followed her until he'd catch himself and pull them away. We all sat together like that well into the night. Loyd and Linda stayed over. Mom gave them her room and moved into mine for the night so I had to sleep with Missy. Jesse's graduation was the only time I ever remember seeing Loyd at one of our school events.

I used to resent this about my dad, that he never bothered to partici-pate in my daily life. I felt that love meant showing up, doing shit you don't always feel like doing. If Loyd loved me, I thought that meant he should pay child support and be around to drive us to school or whatever. And yes, showing up is good parenting, so Loyd wasn't a dependable or responsible father. Thing is, he did love us. He loved us something fierce. And it was an important truth he taught me—that love is not the same as dependability or stability or even safety. The only thing to expect from love is love.

chalet café

LOYD DIDN'T MAKE THE TRIP to The Dalles when I graduated high school. Times were tough, he couldn't miss work, was waiting to get paid. I told him it was fine, made it easy for him to disappoint. He sent me a gift, a gold-plated ring from Fred Meyer Jewelers with a microscopic diamond in it. At the time, I was crazy about Black Hills gold and everyone knew it, so I took Loyd's gift as another insult. If he knew me, he'd know not to buy me a diamond ring. It stayed in its box for a year or so.

After high school, I couldn't really go to college. I'd already been living on my own for part of my senior year so I was really broke. Loyd hadn't filed taxes in years, if ever. Mom had some IRS trouble around that time, to do with Missy's dad, and I couldn't file for financial aid without tax returns from my parents. So I worked full time at Kmart and paid cash to take one community college class at a time. I hung around The Dalles with other kids who were stuck. All of us itched to leave but we didn't have the money or the ambition, or we had family to care for, or some other force keeping us in town. Finally, a friend invited me to share a studio apartment in Bend and go to community college there. I moved with her but couldn't afford classes because rent was so high. I wouldn't have had time for school anyway. I worked mornings at a bakery downtown and afternoons until closing at a coffee shop in the mall.

One month, I was barely getting by and short on rent so I tried to pawn the ring Loyd gave me but the guy said it wasn't worth anything. So I took it to a Fred Meyer Jewelers. I didn't have a receipt so they gave me the lowest possible price, which was $85, not enough to cover my rent. A couple of nights later, I got a little drunk with some friends and spent the money on a bad tattoo.

Bend only lasted a few months. I just couldn't afford it. I moved back to The Dalles, got my job back at Kmart, and started saving. I went along that way, taking classes and saving up and wasting time with other kids who'd been unable to leave town. I got involved with one of my old friends. I'd known Ronnie since seventh grade. He'd never been able to leave town because he'd made a baby in high school. Now he was working at the aluminum plant and learning to let go of the future he'd once imagined for himself. I was pretty sure I'd end up marrying him if I stuck around so I decided to try to get out of town again.

Jesse was in the Coast Guard and stationed in Ketchikan, Alaska. I packed my stuff, gave up my apartment, and took the Alaska Marine Highway north. I moved in with my brother and got a job at a flower shop. There were plenty of Coast Guard guys to party with, but I kept pining over the man I'd left in Oregon. I tried to get into life in Alaska, watched whales and eagles, hiked, and went out on the weekends. I made some fast friends and was never bored but Alaska was tough for me. I missed the sun and worried about my sister. I was so used to keeping an eye on her. When I'd leave to go running Jesse would remind me to watch for bears and, though I loved the endless forest, I was sick of the rain. I didn't even last half a year.

I moved back to The Dalles and stayed with Mom for a couple weeks until I found a place. When I had time in my schedule and enough money, I'd take another class. I had the vague idea I'd get my associate's and move on to a four-year college, but no real plan.

A year or so later, I was sitting next to Ronnie as we drove up Highway 42 toward Camas with his three-year-old, Sol, asleep in the back seat. We'd decided to try to hunt Loyd down to let him know we were getting married. I was fine just letting it go. Having Loyd at the ceremony might make it awkward anyway. But Ronnie insisted we at least try. He said it was just not cool to marry a girl without meeting her dad first. That's just one of the things that I'll always feel grateful to him for.

It was spring. We borrowed Ronnie's dad's Suburban for the trip. We made it into an adventure for Sol, camped in the car, stopped at Enchanted Forest outside of Salem and the animal safari in Winston. Sol had recently asked me, while we sat on the floor building Legos, if I had a daddy. It had been six years since I'd seen Loyd. I told Sol I did have a daddy but he lived far away and I didn't see him very much. Sol was shocked at the idea that a person could live far away from their dad, or not see him very much. And this would be a foundation of my marriage, that my partner was a man who'd never leave or hit his children.

I'd fallen asleep in the car and Ronnie reached over to wake me as we headed up the coastal range. My eyes opened to the familiar trees, the fields, and the camas flowers, purple across the valley. The sun warmed the car and it felt like we were outside of time. I ran my fingers through my hair, pulled it into a fresh ponytail.

The wonder and fear of entering the woods came back to me. I wasn't sure how Loyd might receive us. I'd never introduced him to a boyfriend, so that was one thing. Deeper than that, I was unsure how Loyd might react when he saw Ronnie. Like most white people, I'd always told myself race wasn't a big deal. Character matters, not color, and all that. Only now that I lived with a man who was sometimes asked by strangers where he came from, I'd started to see things that had been in front of my face all along.

Loyd favored towns without streetlights or building codes. Towns where paved roads were few and eventually fed into small dirt lanes or old logging roads. He wasn't a separatist or anti-government. He was just trying to get by. Being a separatist would've required Loyd to actually think about his choices and have opinions about government and politics. Addiction and poverty made it hard for Loyd to get right with the law. If he went to renew his driver's license, they might jail him for outstanding warrants. If he took legitimate work, they'd garnish his wages for child support and unpaid fines. Rental applications required proof of employment. It was just easier to put up a trailer or shack on a remote piece of land and shit in the woods.

Even if his isolation wasn't ideological, Loyd was steeped in a logging culture of mostly white people. And I'm a white person who has lived among white people. I know what sort of talk goes on. As we drove into Loyd's world that day, I thought back with shame to his story about the time I got pneumonia as a baby and he said it was a Hupa curse. I also remembered the way Jesse and I idolized Bo and Luke Duke and their car, the General Lee. I'd clutched the Matchbox version, confederate symbol in my sweaty palm, and never knew better as I sang out the first few notes of Dixie every time I made that car pull off some awesome stunt.

I'd never heard Loyd say much about race. He liked to think he chose friends because they were hardworking and up for a good time. No doubt he was prone to a certain brand of racism. We all are, one way or another. If I tried hard, I thought maybe I heard old echoes of talk of a brown man on a logging crew. *Got a newbie on the crew, Mexican or Indian or somethin', and man alive if he isn't a hardworkin' sonofabitch. Can hold his beers, too, so he's alright with me.* Back in our migrating days, I probably would've thought something like this was nice for Loyd to say, a compliment that felt Sesame Street–approved. I wouldn't know then to cringe at the assumption that Loyd's approval should matter to the new man, the idea that he stood in judgment and the man had to pass some test. When I brought my new family to meet him, I wasn't worried about Loyd's approval. I was worried he might say something ignorant or insulting. And I was mad at myself for not thinking of it before we made the trip.

I knew Loyd and Linda were back in Camas Valley, but as usual I didn't have an address for them. Jesse had been to their place and tried giving me directions. He used all these valley landmarks but I didn't know what he meant by half of them. I guess I'd never paid enough attention to learn the right names. I'd scratched down notes while we talked on the phone, but they didn't make any sense to me as we approached town so I decided we'd just drive straight to the Chalet. I was worried memory might not even get me there but you can't drive through Camas Valley and miss the

Chalet café. It sits right on the highway. Even if Linda wasn't working there anymore, I figured someone at the Chalet would be able to tell us where to find her and Loyd.

When I saw the Chalet, something shifted in my chest. It looked the same, but my impression was different. As a kid, I loved going to the Chalet. It had one of those claw machines and I got soda and French fries. Now I realized that, from the outside, it looked like a place you might not want to take children. The windows were darkened by red textured plastic, I guess meant to look like stained glass. If you saw it from the side, where we were parked, it might be a tavern or even a strip club. But the front had wide windows facing the highway and filling the dining area with sunlight. I wondered what Ronnie thought. The Chalet was his first real look at Loyd's world.

I didn't get out of the car right away. I double-knotted my off-white Converse low tops, anxiety spreading in my belly. I pulled the visor down and checked myself in the mirror. Pulled out the ponytail, ran my fingers through my hair, put it back. Sol was still waking.

Why don't I go in and ask, I said. You can let Sol finish waking up? Ronnie agreed and that was a relief. I had little experience mixing Loyd with anyone from my regular life. It suddenly occurred to me to wonder what Ronnie would see when I spoke to Loyd. I knew I'd drop my g's, say *ain't*. I hadn't seen Loyd in so long, I should give him that.

I opened the car door and stepped down, running it in my head. Even if Linda wasn't there, I was afraid of how I might be received. To Loyd's friends, I was always the longed-for daughter, the child whose life was too busy and sophisticated for her logger daddy. Stretching after the long drive, I wondered if Linda was in the café right now, delivering a French dip to somebody sitting at a booth with red vinyl benches. I wondered what she'd do when she saw me. I sometimes felt she had an impulse to protect Loyd from the heartache I caused.

The Chalet door swung open and a dirty logger stepped out. It was late afternoon, just that time when a farm laborer or timber man might've finished his work and gone to the Chalet for a meal and a little company. That time of day when the sun hangs a moment, as it falls back toward earth, at just the right angle to let magic in through the sky. I closed the car door and faced the man leaving the café. It's strange that my first thought at seeing this man, with his thick dungarees and flannel shirt, his steel-toed boots and faded baseball cap, was *logger*, not *Loyd*. Strange because it was my dad who now paused, noticed me, and held the door open for the young lady walking toward him. He looked up in pleasant greeting, a smile for a stranger. I met his eye and his smile lost its confidence. He wasn't sure but I was. He'd filled out a little but it was Loyd. I spoke first.

Hi Daddy.

He dropped the door, his eyes instantly wet. He always felt so much more than he could say. He took a couple of loud, familiar breaths.

Sweetheart? He looked at me more closely then shot his eyes to the car I'd come from.

Hi Daddy, I repeated.

And we did what we always did. Like riding a bike. Like packing a saw out of the woods. Like swimming in a warm summer lake. He held me and I felt his tears on my temple and he drew a deep, slow breath, tried to control his sob.

What a nice surprise, he choked out.

Time was frozen again and it was a pure moment.

Because the truth is you can have those sometimes, even after the worst betrayal or assault. Trauma doesn't dismantle love and logic has no place in the complicated loyalties we give our parents. It felt like a miracle that he'd walked out just as we pulled up. That he'd held the door for a stranger, maybe even thought to himself, *she kinda looks like Tina*, something I'd often thought when I saw men of his build and walk of life. I don't know. I only know he could've left the Chalet two minutes earlier or we could've pulled up two minutes later, but that's not what happened. Like so many of my moments with my dad, this one played out as if choreographed.

It was hard to let go. This was the first honest, innocent embrace I'd shared with Loyd since Packwood. I didn't want to pull my face from his warm shirt, to leave the sawdust and gasoline smell, the familiar way he held me so tight it hurt. I'd known that smell and the pressure of those arms my whole life, the song of my joints cracking from the strength of my dad's hold. When I was running out of breath, I pulled myself together and stepped back.

I told him why we'd come and who was in the car with me. Sol was watching from the back seat, his head stretched out to look past his dad. I walked over to pick him up. When he was sleepy or nervous, Sol used to take a strand of my hair and put it in his mouth while he laid his head on my shoulder. He did so now. It was an odd habit and Loyd noticed. It seemed to tell him all he needed to know about the new family I was making.

Ronnie walked up to Loyd and offered his hand. Loyd shook it, looked Ronnie over, and put his hand on his shoulder. A warm smile lit up Loyd's eyes.

Nice shoes, was all he said. Ronnie and Sol were both wearing classic black converse. Ronnie high tops, Sol low tops, both black with white soles and laces. Loyd pretty much always wore simple black and white converse when he wasn't wearing steel-toed boots.

Loyd asked if we were hungry and insisted we go into the Chalet, where he had just finished eating, and let him buy us a meal. He went to find Linda as soon as we stepped inside. We were waiting in the dim doorway when they came back. She was wearing a stained, white apron and wiping her hands on a dishtowel, her sideways smile growing as she walked. It was a genuine smile and it revealed a sort of melancholic love. I could always feel that she had true affection for me but was also cautious of me. I'm sure my visits always came with emotional consequences for Loyd. I could sense that she was already considering the aftermath of this one.

Still, she smiled her crooked smile, arranged to hide her missing teeth, and welcomed us. Linda hadn't aged, but she was thinner. She held my face and ran her hands down my long ponytail to land on my shoulders. Linda's eyes were always so full of something I didn't understand. She often held my eyes longer than was comfortable and it seemed she was trying to tell me something I was too stupid to puzzle out. Looking Linda in the eyes was like standing in front of a brilliant painting. I wanted to understand, to be educated about the layers of meaning, but I think that would take a lifetime. The colors and lines shift with the light.

Loyd asked Linda to give us *the best seat in the house*. She led us to a booth and gave us each a menu in a plastic folder. Loyd stopped along the way, letting folks know his daughter was in town to share good news, she came from six hours away, *she's getting married to this fella here and this little guy is my grandkid.*

Hey, meet my grandson.

There are things I didn't know yet, things I know now, that change this scene for me. When I was with Loyd in the Chalet that day, I didn't know yet that he was not Jesse's biological father. Now, I wonder if it was on Loyd's mind that day, if he noticed this parallel between my life and his. He'd married a person who already had a very young son, just as I was about to do. He'd accepted the role of that child's parent without condition, just as I did. He fathered Jesse so wholly that I was shocked when I learned the truth. I always thought Jesse was Loyd's favorite child, which I didn't hold against him. Jesse was my hero. They certainly had more in common and spent more time together. My point is that Loyd loved Jesse fiercely and this moment in the Chalet, the way he immediately claimed Sol, is the only moment I can ever find as evidence that Loyd had adopted Jesse. He was able to make this child his family in an instant.

Sol clung tightly to me as we sat down to eat lunch. He was still waking, still warming to Loyd and the whole situation. Loyd loved the energy of kids but Sol was mellow, thoughtful. Not the rowdy sort of boy Loyd understood. Sol was fascinated with machines so I told him that my daddy cut down trees for his job. He asked if Loyd had a chainsaw. They soon found they had plenty of common ground in the area of body humor. At first Loyd was hesitant, probably remembering how Mom forbid using the word "puke" at the table and worried I might have the same sort of rules. I did not. By the time lunch arrived, Sol was telling Loyd all about how he was learning to spell. We'd figured out he was more motivated if he was having fun. His first spelling word was "butt," which he spelled for Loyd now.

Butt. B.U.T.T. Butt, he giggled as Linda set a grilled cheese in front of him and snorted at Loyd's glee. Sol moved on to "poop."

P.O.O.P. Poop.

OK, food's on the table so how about we take the poop off the table? I could hear my mother in my voice. Loyd's eyes were shining as he watched us together.

After eating, we went to Loyd and Linda's place. Dad wanted to show off his garden and send us home with some veggies. We followed the Pinto west on 42 and turned down a dirt road called Hard Cash Lane. Loyd drove clear to the end of the rutted road, where they lived in the back corner of somebody's property. The place on Hard Cash Lane was even more elaborate than his place in Packwood all those years ago. He had perfected his own style of self-made housing. I'm not sure what his arrangement was with the landowner—he probably did odd jobs for them to pay for using up a corner of their land. I didn't know it then, but this would be Loyd's last home.

When I picture Loyd in the valley, I'll always picture him at the place on Hard Cash Lane. He started with an abandoned sixteen-foot camper trailer and built a huge structure beside it, so the trailer door opened up into this extra room. This shack, made mostly of scrap lumber, tripled the square footage of the trailer, which was really nice for him and Linda in the winter months when they couldn't sit out in lawn chars for their morning coffee and afternoon beer. The shack's floor was covered in green carpet and it had a small woodstove against one wall faced by an old couch. A small black and white TV with rabbit ears sat in the corner. Behind the trailer was a gas-powered generator for cooking and running the TV when they could afford fuel.

I have a pretty good understanding of how Loyd built this compound because he documented the process with his camera. He took aerial photos during construction and that's pretty amazing, considering he did it all himself, including the photography. Loyd strung the camera around his neck, put on his old logging spikes, and climbed some of the giant Doug firs surrounding the place. He's easily fifty feet up in some of the shots.

Linda wanted to get a picture of Loyd in those treetops but never could because he had the camera up there with him. In some, you can see Linda below, her hand over her eyes to block the sun, as she looks up toward Loyd, anxious he might fall.

He must've gone up a few different times to take the photos. There are shots of early staging, pre-construction. Lines dug in the dirt to indicate layout. Then there are shots of the shack partially framed, some of the garden structures already built. The shack framed up with no walls, the shack with walls, and the shack with roof. In each new wave of photos the garden has grown, the plants getting bigger, then flowering and producing by the time the place was all built.

The kitchen was signature Loyd. Salvaged plywood, scrap lumber, and hand-cut logs. A countertop Loyd cobbled together, nine or ten feet long with wooden boxes stacked up at the back to make a sort of cabinetry. He covered the surface of the countertop with an old carpet remnant in mottled brown oranges. On top of the carpet are several cutting boards of various sizes.

He led us to the sitting area sprinkled with seating options. Mostly lawn chairs, mismatched in style and era. There was a fuzzy brown recliner and a wicker throne with a tall, fan-like back and blue seat cushion. There was a horseshoe pit with a picnic table off to the side.

Rustic pillars stood here and there. He made them by splitting logs in thirds or quarters lengthwise. He'd sink them into the ground until they were unmovable. Some were placed to allow for temporary tarp roofing that could be draped across, so they could sit or cook outside in the rain. Some of the pillars had spikes hanging off them to store garden tools, net potato sacks Linda brought home from the café, buckets, rope, bungee cords. Everything had a purpose.

Loyd grew a ton of produce on that plot and could trade it around town for things they needed. Or just give it away, which he loved to do. Sharing gave him an opportunity to show off his garden, and helped him bank goodwill among the townspeople, which came in handy during lean times. He usually hand watered his garden, even though there was a water spigot out there. When his plants were just seedlings, he'd fill a bucket and carry it around, scooping water out with a paper cup and squatting at each plant. This way, he didn't waste and he could check on all his plants as they grew. He designed the garden with little trenches that ran along next to his plants so he could put the hose at the end of each row and irrigate the garden as it grew and needed more water. Once the really hot days hit, he'd break down and use a sprinkler from time to time, to cool the garden down a bit. But he preferred the meditation of hand watering.

We sat there and visited until long after Linda came home from her shift at the Chalet. She'd asked another waitress for a ride since they only had the one car and Loyd normally came to get her. Loyd was tickled when I told him I'd given up my job at Kmart to become a florist. He felt connected to that somehow, like all the garden chores he'd assigned in childhood led me to flowers. I think he was imagining me working at a nursery, not arranging wedding bouquets. I didn't correct him. He was right to think that his forced garden tending had left an imprint on me. Ronnie sat there looking at Loyd's garden in wonder.

Loyd, he said, I see a smaller version of your garden in my backyard every day.

He told Loyd I was always digging out paths and heaping the extra dirt into beds just the same odd way. That each zucchini plant was given exactly the same sort of mound, all to itself, and how all the zucchinis were grouped together in a little village, just like his. Like Loyd, I grew nasturtiums and marigolds to keep pests out. I built Sol a small fort out of branches and grew morning glory on it. I even woke him early on a summer morning and carried him out to see how they're most lovely first thing, that's how they get their name.

Loyd teared up hard, hearing Ronnie describe how I staked my plants and built supports out of gathered sticks instead of buying tomato cages or trellises from the store. I'd honestly not considered it before but he was right. My vegetable garden was a smaller version of Loyd's. They were similar in the same way my handwriting looks like my mom's. Almost everything I knew about how to care for my garden I'd learned from my dad, but there was his intrinsic visual aesthetic, too. When Ronnie finished, Loyd just took it all in for a little while. He was in awe of the people sitting with him and we shared a comfortable silence while we watched the sun lower in the sky.

When it started to get dark, we wound down to our goodbyes. We had about an hour's drive to our hotel. Loyd just kept repeating how proud he was and what a great surprise it had been to see me in front of the Chalet like that. He loaded us up with produce from his garden, and I didn't mention our own full garden at home. I knew it was important to Loyd, that he be able to give me some of his bounty. He asked us to give some 'maters to my mom. When he mentioned Mom, his eyes told anyone looking that he still loved her.

I bet she'll like this one, he said, it's one of them fancy heirloom types. When he said *heirloom* he tossed his nose up and to the right, lifted his hand in a flourish, pinky up. Loyd couldn't say a word like that without acknowledging it didn't really belong in his mouth.

By the time we left, Ronnie had adapted his language to Loyd just as well as I did. Now that I think about it, that shouldn't have been a surprise. Ronnie worked at the aluminum plant with other men who, like Loyd, were most comfortable when working. When your life is a string of hardships, it can be hard to find value in polite talk. Plus Ronnie grew up in a bilingual household. He knew all about changing his talk when he needed to. It was a relief to see him do it because I'd always thought I was some kind of poser, changing myself like that. Watching Ronnie, I saw how sincere his effort was. His only motive was to connect, to create understanding between them. Loyd shook Ronnie's hand goodbye.

I promise I'll take good care of your daughter, Ronnie said.

It was old-fashioned and patriarchal, but also just the kind of thing Loyd needed to hear. It gave the illusion of passing off his fatherly duties, made it easier to ignore all the years his daughter had to take care of herself.

I knew it the minute I saw your shoes, Loyd replied. He held onto Ronnie's hand while he said it. Patted him on the shoulder with his free hand, pulling Ronnie into a side hug. It was funny because Loyd was a much smaller man. When it was my turn, Loyd held me a good long time before he let me go. We got into the car, that familiar lump swelling up in my throat.

Your dad's rad, Ronnie said as we drove away down Hard Cash Lane.

(((

Loyd called me a week or so before our wedding to say he wouldn't make it. The generator quit so he'd have to work his ass off to have enough cash to buy another before fall came. I wasn't surprised and didn't dwell on it. Caught up in the drama and energy of young adulthood, I was building a new life with a sense of urgency and clouded vision. I couldn't see how Loyd and his absence shaped all my choices. I thought I was building a road to a new reality and I was, but I didn't take any time to consider where I actually wanted it to go. It was a road built in one direction—away from what I'd known.

Before Loyd even called I'd already asked Mom to walk me down the aisle. It felt right and I was a little worried how I'd explain that if he did show up. But I never really considered it a true possibility. This was how Loyd loved me, by removing himself. I didn't really see it that way at the time, but I'd at least come to the idea that it was more than just not wanting to be there. I understood Loyd was doing what he felt was easier for all of us by staying away. And because he'd done it so long, it really was easier without him.

(((

I returned to the place on Hard Cash Lane a couple years later with Jesse. When I called to tell Jesse I was expecting a baby, his wife, Tammy, was already six months pregnant. Our babies would be just three months apart. Jesse suggested we make the trip to tell Loyd in person he was going to have two new grandkids. Jesse called ahead and left word at the Chalet that we were coming to town, so this time Loyd was expecting us. We spent another day sitting in chairs looking at Loyd's garden and talking about the two babies on the way. Loyd was pretty excited about the whole thing

and wondered if maybe next time we'd all sit here together with a couple
of babies getting into everything. Jesse already knew he was having a son
but I'd decided to be surprised. I felt I would have a daughter but it wasn't
verified by any tests. I ended up being right. What I didn't imagine was that
she'd never meet Loyd. I didn't know that this would be the last time I ever
saw my dad alive.

❮ ❮ ❮

Loyd called me from the Chalet in late December 1999. He wanted to say
he loved me and wished he'd done better. This was just in case Y2K was real
and the world ended.

Now, I don't usually buy into that sort of bullshit, honey. But just in
case I wanted to let you know Daddy loves you more than anything.

When he said that, I felt five years old again. But I also I had a new sort
of understanding for his anxiety. I was pregnant and raising a son. I'd come
to know the sort of morbid fantasies that come with loving your children,
the way nothing feels as ugly or scary as not being able to keep them safe.
How terrifying it is to think they may not know you love them.

❮ ❮ ❮

The last time I talked to my dad was in late February 2000. It was about a
week after my daughter, Lillian, was born. Loyd called because Linda had
put my due date on the calendar and they'd been watching the days pass,
wondering if my baby was OK. Lillian was a week late so I can see how
they'd be worried. I was touched to realize they were waiting to hear, to
know that they'd been anticipating her. I pictured Loyd pacing the floor,
wondering. And I felt guilty because it hadn't occurred to me to call my
dad. I was exhausted by joy and hunting him down was always so much
work.

I gave Loyd the basic baby stats, which I had to repeat, slowly, a few
times so he could relay them to Linda, who was writing it all down. I told
him about the way Sol had been sleeping in our room every night because
he didn't want to be too far from his baby sister, how he came home from

kindergarten every day and held her. How he'd been jealous when his little friend, Ian, noticed that her name, *Lillian*, had *Ian* in it. The boys had asked how to spell the baby's name.

L.I.L.L.I.A.N. Wait! That has IAN in it!

No it does not, Sol cried. She's MY sister. After that, Sol preferred we use her shortened name. Lily. Loyd liked that, said he'd have to get some lilies in the garden.

I told Loyd stories I hoped would delight him and give him something to say to his friends, to Aunt Rainy and Uncle Papa. But there was a lot I didn't say.

I wish I'd told Loyd about the pain and the power of childbirth, the way my body knew what to do. How I'd figured out that the things that hurt can also make us mighty. I think that's something he could have related to. I wish I'd told him how I thought about that steelhead from Packwood when I was in labor, his fish body made only of muscle and the way he struggled with the entire force of his life toward a singular purpose. I wish I'd told Loyd that the terror, blood, and joy of childbirth made me think there might be life after death. If birth can happen every day, anything is possible. And I wish I'd told him that this was something he'd often shown me—that pain isn't the worst thing. Would I be able to ride a bike without it? To swim? To let my children go someday? *If I ain't hurtin', I ain't livin'.*

Those two phone calls would become deeply significant to me. I tell myself they both say so much about Loyd. The Y2K call shows that making sure I knew I was loved was life-and-death important to him. He wanted to hear my voice when he thought the world might end. And it carries some of the whimsical humor I loved about Loyd, that he couldn't be counted on to remember my birthday but he was damn-well gonna call me in case of apocalypse.

The second showed concern for Lillian, the new girl child, his only genetic heir besides me. She'd never meet him in person but Loyd has shaped her whole life, in good ways and bad. My overprotective tendencies, my pushing to make sure Lillian is free and strong. But she'd never be in his physical presence. All she gets is that phone call, that moment when he reached out across the distance between us to settle his mind that she was healthy and had come safely to this world.

It never occurred to me then, but even her name feels connected to Loyd. I was born in Headquarters, the end of the Camas Prairie Railroad. Loyd died in Camas Valley. These two opposite poles in the boundaries of Loyd's territory, a couple hundred miles apart, seem unconnected. But they're both home to native Camas flower. It's a plant that was important to indigenous people, its root a food source. Sometimes called the camas lily, its flower welcomes spring in both places. I didn't know all that when we named our daughter.

I can't even say why, but I wish Loyd had held Lily. I'd never leave my kids in Loyd's care or want Lily to date a man like him. Still, if I could change one thing, I'm not sure I'd erase the violence or the vandalism, the abandonment or even the kiss. If I only got one shot to change my story of Loyd, I'd probably make sure I took the time to carry my daughter into the woods just once, so she could feel her grandpa holding her, put her head against his chest and know his sawdust and cigarette smell. Let her feel that singular sense of being holy as I had when I was young.

other sheep

I DIDN'T HAVE SOME MAGIC SENSE when Loyd died. I didn't suddenly feel a sawdust-scented wind on my face or hear a distant chainsaw and think of my dad. For a couple of hours my dad was dead and I had no idea. It was June 21, 2001. One month and one day before Loyd's forty-ninth birthday, which I likely would have failed to acknowledge. I was hosting a barbeque, a belated Father's Day celebration for Ronnie and his dad. Father's Day had been the weekend before and I hadn't called the Chalet or sent Loyd a card or anything.

It was sunny and lovely outside so we were all sitting around the picnic table in my backyard. My mom was running late so she wasn't there yet when Ronnie answered the phone and brought it to me.

It's your brother.

Jesse lives too far away to make gatherings like this but he is ridiculously good at calling on holidays or times when the family is together and he can't be with us. We always pass the phone around, give updates on kids, jobs, household repairs. So it was normal for Jesse to call but I was surprised because this wasn't an actual holiday and I didn't recall telling him we were gathering. I thought maybe Mom had. I took the phone.

Hello?

How's it going? Jesse pretty much always starts with this.

Good, just finally getting together for the dads. Did you have a good

Father's Day? I got up from the picnic table and went to the kitchen so I could finish getting dinner ready.

Oh yeah, I always get spoiled, he said. So, you have company?

Yeah, just Ronnie's folks. Mom's on her way.

I didn't mention she was late because her husband had decided not to come at the last minute. He loved to make her choose on days like this.

Do you think you could step away for a minute? Jesse asked. Maybe into the other room or something?

Background chatter stopped and the summer sun went cool through the kitchen window. Why should my brother need to talk about something that requires privacy? Or even a serious tone?

Sure. I walked into the hallway before asking, What's up?

Well, I just got a call from Linda.

Holy shit. We'd never, in all the years, received a phone call from Linda. I didn't say anything at first. I stayed quiet and walked up the stairs to my bedroom, the most private place I could go. I shut the door behind me. I remember thinking maybe Loyd was in the hospital. I remember wondering how he'd pay for a hospital stay, if somehow his children could be held responsible. I pictured a chainsaw injury, a mangled limb.

OK. I'm upstairs. I sat on my bed. I'm alone. Why's Linda calling?

Jesse waited. Maybe he wanted me to have a dad for a couple more minutes.

Well, because I guess Dad died today.

These were magic words with the power to transform us. Before Jesse said them, I was a mother and wife, a college student and a school board member. Jesse was a husband and a father who lived hours away from me. But once he spoke those words, we travelled together through time. The years between our childhood forests and our adult lives evaporated. I was that little girl again, prepared to follow my brother through something so enormous and terrifying I couldn't see the end of it.

My first thought was that my birthday was coming. It was fitting. Loyd was always causing a disturbance around my birthday. We were usually either already with him, or starting our summer visit and leaving Mom around that time. All my life I'd associated my birthday with him and with heartache. But it was also fitting because it was so unexpected and dramatic. An eruption in the middle of a peaceful summer day. And it was tragic because he was so young. It all just fit.

My second thought was of Mom. How grateful I was for her tireless rule—the only truly inflexible rule in her book. Always hug each other, always say *I love you* when you say goodbye. I can be sure, without any doubt, that the last thing I ever told my dad was that I loved him.

Jesse waited on the phone. I don't think either of us knew how to step into this reality. This moment is one I can recall with perfect clarity. It was that magic hour that happens late in a summer afternoon, sun streaming in through my window and hitting the wood floor to create a soft, honey glow. Dust floated in that beam of light, dancing like a million happy creatures untouched by my personal tragedy. I'd just recently convinced Sol that dust motes like these were tiny fairies flying around in warm sunshine. I could hear Sol's voice out back, encouraging Lily to say the names of the small plastic animals she was clutching in her hands. *Lily, remember? Hooorssse. Tiiigerr.* She had dozens of them and was always sorting them out. Sol had been teaching her their names and he wanted her to perform for their grandparents.

I wasn't sure how to move out of the moment, wasn't sure I wanted to. The family on my patio didn't know I'd been transformed. I didn't want my sorrow to touch them. Ronnie came looking for me. I asked him if Mom had shown up yet, asked him to send her up as soon as she did. All I wanted now was my mom.

Because Mom was among the very few people who could understand my relationship with my dad. Loyd was one of those things you can only appreciate if you witness it yourself, like a riot, or an earthquake, or a sunset so red it makes you want to believe in God. He can't really be explained.

I knew my mom would mourn him and that she'd understand my complicated grief. I've heard soldiers sometimes crave the company of other soldiers because nobody else, no matter how close, can understand where they've been the way another soldier can. Nobody else can know the terror and beauty of their specific war. I needed Mom because she knew the warmth of Loyd's singular brand of unconditional love and the scorching flame that love could ignite. Like me, she had both loved Loyd and survived him.

Obituaries always say, "he is survived by," before listing the living family members of the dead. When I say we survived Loyd, I don't just mean we lived longer than him. I mean we survived him the way you survive a hurricane or a car accident. You might be injured and you've probably learned some terrible lessons, but you're still kicking. He hurt us, but we made it. And there were things we missed about him. Certain beauties can only be seen in the complication of hardship. There were things we learned about repair and recovery, things we couldn't have learned any other way. Nobody would choose an earthquake or car accident, but the experience shapes you, simple as that.

I could wish for a different dad, but that's like driftwood wishing it never had to touch the ocean. Without floating in the salt and waves, it wouldn't be driftwood at all. To wish away my hard times is to wish away parts of myself. And beyond all that, I still held on to the notion that I'd do more than simply survive Loyd. I had this foolish hope that I'd get to enjoy a functional relationship with Loyd, on my own terms, now that I was an adult. That I'd find a way to get the good things from my dad, ask him to build my kids a playhouse and help with my garden, without fear now because I was grown and no longer powerless to adults.

Because, despite the whole long, exhausting shit-show that was Loyd's life, there was so much creativity and joy that came along with it. There was a reason Linda stuck with him all those years and Mom always said he was *The One* and I still called him daddy when I spoke to him. Loyd had his demons, no doubt. But so much of this life is learning to live with your monsters. My dad was only one of my monsters and he wasn't even the scariest. He was just the one I loved the most. I couldn't accept that I'd just survive him. I wanted more than that, felt like I'd earned more.

Linda told Jesse that Loyd collapsed while working for a local farmer. He went fast. The farmer called an ambulance but Loyd was gone before it got there. Linda wanted us to come help manage everything. Because they'd divorced all those years before, she was worried maybe she had no legal claim to Loyd's body. He'd been taken to a funeral home in Winston. We needed to decide what to do with him.

We brought our families along to Camas Valley. Once again we borrowed the big Suburban, this time because it fit everyone. We got a hotel room with a pool for the kids and drove a half hour each day to the valley. Linda held the babies and talked with Sol about first grade. She looked wrung out. I kept trying to feed her but she wasn't hungry. We sat around watching Hunter and Lily toddle around Loyd's garden, getting dirty and putting everything in their mouths. Whenever they did something silly or cute, Linda would make her airy little burst of a laugh and click her tongue. I could see that, all those years, what I'd interpreted as annoyance or impatience from Linda was actually admiration and delight. I wondered how many other things I'd gotten wrong.

After a few days, Ronnie and Tammy took the kids home. Ronnie was in trade school while working full time. He couldn't miss more class and we couldn't afford missed wages. We also couldn't pay to keep renting hotel rooms so an old friend of Uncle Papa's took us in. He had a big double-wide with a family room where Jess and I slept on the couches. His wife kept us fed and he loaned us a car so we could get around town. Mom said she'd drive down to get us when we were ready to head home.

We spent a sunny afternoon with Linda, sitting on the mismatched chairs outside their place and talking about Loyd. Sitting there, it was pretty hard to believe Loyd wasn't in the world anymore. He surrounded us. The shack he built, that had sheltered him and Linda through hard winters and hot summers. The garden he'd fed them from. Loyd had imagined and built the entire thing, it was his creature. I couldn't see how Linda would maintain any of it without him. Loyd was the blood that ran through this homestead, giving life and keeping order as he moved through its spaces. It was an organism, a breathing thing. Every single day Loyd tweaked and tinkered, added and took away. It couldn't go on living without its creator.

Linda kept offering us Dad's things. I took a pair of steel-toed rain boots. They were too big but I thought maybe I could wear them to work in my yard. Loyd went on a long walk in the woods every day and picked up treasures. He'd collected a bunch of antler sheds and I said I'd take a few. A cactus in a short, round terra cotta pot sat on the edge of his garden. I wanted something living from Loyd so I took the cactus and dug up some baby trees from overcrowded clumps in the surrounding forest. The saplings all died but the cactus is still happy. It's survived a couple of moves and drops little babies in the garden bed around its pot. I sometimes forget while I'm weeding and end up with a handful of tiny, irritating spines I have to dig out with tweezers.

At one point, Linda got up and went inside. She brought out a white, rectangular box made of that shiny cardboard meant for the freezer. It was a restaurant-sized corndog box. Many of Loyd and Linda's storage containers were bulk food packaging she brought home from the café. The corndog box was full of photos. She told us to take whatever we wanted. This is where I discovered so many of the photos I didn't know Linda had taken.

We each grabbed a handful to go through. We'd pass them around, try to decide when or where each had been taken, how old we were, what town we were in. Me and Jesse, shirtless and wet, standing in front of the slip-n-slide Loyd made by staking out a long sheet of black plastic in the lawn of a rented cottage in Randle. Me and Jesse standing in front of the giant crows at the Yard Birds in Chehalis. Loyd and Uncle Papa, holding Rainier beers up to the camera in the Blue Tarp Inn. Linda wasn't in many of the pictures. She held the camera and we let her disappear.

Jesse pulled out a picture with rounded edges and laughed, handing it to me.

Remember this, dork?

It was a photo of one of those childhood mishaps Loyd had turned into folklore. Even if I'd been too young to remember, Loyd retold it enough that I knew the history as soon as I saw the picture.

I'm crying in the photo. I'm maybe four or five years old, wearing a favorite light purple sweatshirt, tattered around the neck and sleeves. The photo was taken in Clallam Bay, near the firepit outside the double-wide where my parent's marriage came to its violent end. Looking at the picture, I could feel Loyd behind the camera, how angry I was when it flashed.

We'd roasted hot dogs for dinner that night, sitting around the fire with our own roasting sticks. It was coming up on bedtime. Waves crashed below the bluff and I was staring into the embers. It was fascinating, the way wood burned orange then turned black. Fires mellowed me out, made me thoughtful. Loyd was the same way. Neither of us cared to talk much around a fire. For me, it was like staring at wood paneling or a cloudy sky, looking for shapes and turning them into stories. Campfire shapes always change so the stories can go anywhere. I never thought to ask Loyd if he was playing the same game when he stared into a fire.

I was sleepy, my eyes on the fire, when the wind changed and I got a serious face full of smoke. Loyd sensed it coming just an instant before and called out for me to turn my head but it was too late. The assault was sudden and painful, like a bee sting. My eyes burned like the fire itself had jumped into them. I cried right away. Loyd bolted over and scooped me up into clean air. It felt good to be rescued. But just when I started to calm, he got to laughing. *Sweetheart, Daddy couldn't help it. I laughed so hard I thought I'd bust a gut because you was cryin' the biggest tears I ever seen.*

He set me down on the picnic table and I waited for the feel of his rough thumbs wiping away my tears, a tender scraping I'd always known. Instead, he reached for his camera. *You were soakin' wet from them crocodile tears and I ain't pullin' your leg!* He'd beam right here in the story, as if I'd accomplished something and we all needed to take a moment to appreciate that. *Daddy just had to take a picture so you could see how big those suckers were!*

I wanted to be held. I wanted sympathy. Taking my picture felt cruel. So I started crying even harder. Every time Loyd told this story, it was like he was still trying to convince me how funny it was. He was molding my experience, hoping to reshape my feelings about it.

Well Tina Marie, now you weren't just hurtin'. You were mad as hell. You had that pissed off cry goin' but Daddy just knew you'd be glad I took it when that picture came back. I mean these tears were big enough for a tadpole to go swimmin' in!

So he took the picture. When he set the camera down, I demanded he do something to stop my pain.

It hurts, Daddy. Fix it!

Honey, he said, I know how that feels and I wouldn't wish it on nobody. Smoke in your eyes stings somethin' fierce. But Daddy can't fix it. Just close your peepers and hold on a bit. Sometimes, only thing to do is wait for the hurt to stop.

I dug my knuckles into my eye sockets but he pulled my hands away.

Just keep 'em closed, he said. Ain't nothin' for it but time.

I don't remember that picture coming back developed or how I reacted when it did. It doesn't really capture my giant tears anyway. You can tell I'm crying but the tears look unremarkable. Still, I'm grateful now that Loyd took the picture. When Jesse handed it to me that day on Hard Cash Lane, it felt like I was experiencing string theory, stepping over a wrinkle in time. I could almost convince myself Loyd had created the wrinkle with intention, to reach out and speak to me across the wall that separates the living from the dead.

I held the photo in my hand and looked around me. My brother was waiting, I still hadn't responded to his taunt. *Remember this, dork?* We were figuring out the dynamics of our shared grief, how to approach all the unsayable things set before us with Loyd's sudden death. We were in the forest once again, facing the unknown together. Jesse assumed the role of capable eldest, laughing everything off, acting like it wasn't a big deal. And I was again the fussy baby, lingering over every injury, asking the questions out loud that everybody else seemed to know were best left unasked.

Linda was watching me too, as I stared at the photo and processed this memory from before she came into our lives. Sitting there on another summer day, in another of the places Loyd built to keep his family warm and dry, another of the many homes I'd been ashamed of, always ashamed, Loyd's wisdom came back to me on the breeze.

I hadn't thought of his words in years, if ever. *Ain't nothin' for it but time.* But he'd said them often as I grew. *Only thing you can do is wait for the hurt to stop.* I thought of Paul Bunyan, sitting next to the campfire alone after he buried Babe in the grave he dug, five miles wide, in the Black

Hills. How lonesome he felt, how unchangeable his fate. *Ain't nothin' for it but time.*

It was a lesson Loyd taught me countless ways. Pain passes. Nothing lasts forever, not campfires or summer visits, not bloody fights or unwanted kisses. Not my dad. Everything is eventually swallowed up by time.

I repeated my dad's words to myself, like a mantra, the whole time I was in the valley. As Jesse and I went through his things, arranged his service, buried his ashes. Every task brought a new wave of grief, a renewal of that aching sense of abandonment, this time permanent. The possibility of Loyd's redemption was gone and all our unfinished business would be his legacy. As we learned to navigate this new kind of fatherlessness, I just kept telling myself the same thing. Tina, ain't nothing for this but time.

(((((((((

I asked Jesse to take me to see the place where Loyd died. It's a field as beautiful as a painting. I remember thinking, when I saw it, that most people would want to die in a place like that.

Today, I'm standing at my kitchen counter writing about that place and it occurs to me that there's symmetry this kitchen shares with that field. The counter I'm standing at is a huge blond slab of butcher block and it looks over the sunken dining room below, framed on all sides by tall windows looking out into my green yard. It's a room I feel I don't exactly deserve. Or maybe deserve is the wrong word, I guess it sort of feels like a room for somebody else. The room, the yard, the shrubs I've planted, the wood floor we installed, the two little dogs alert at the glass door, waiting for the squirrel to run by again so they can continue the important work of letting me know about it. It all feels like it validates me somehow. Like this is the room, the house, of a person who deserves to take up space in the world. A productive person who does more harm than good. That's how Loyd's field feels, like a sort of validation. I can't help but think this beautiful death means something. Maybe he earned it somehow, maybe he had merit the universe recognized.

The farmer who'd hired Loyd that day agreed to see me. He took me to the field and I asked if he could show me where Loyd fell, the exact place. He paced around a bit, like a dog sniffing around, deciding where to take a nap. He stopped when he found the spot and waited for me to come take his place.

To me, this was an incredible kindness. I think Jesse thought it was a bit much—needing to go to the field at all. But the farmer seemed to understand what I needed from it. Maybe he wanted to share it, too. Pass on a bit of the weight he'd carried since watching Loyd die. I stood in Loyd's spot and listened as the farmer told me about his death.

He said it was coming up on quitting time and all the sudden Loyd just stopped cold, stood straight as a board and looked up, like he heard something in the sky. Next thing he was on the ground. Just like that. He couldn't find Loyd's pulse but he called 911 anyway.

Standing in Loyd's place, I took in the view. I didn't lie down or anything, didn't take it that far. I just stood in the spot and lifted my face, as I imagined he had, to look ahead. The last thing Loyd ever saw in this world was incredible beauty.

For a long time after he died, I couldn't stop imagining it. I was pretty sure I could see everything just like it happened. Even when I met the farmer, he felt familiar. The shadow of his figure already loomed in the background of my fantasy of Loyd's death. My dad would never tell me the story of that day in the field. This piece of history was mine to carry and a lifetime of Loyd's stories had given me everything I needed to imagine it for myself.

I could picture him. I knew he wore tattered Lee jeans or thick canvas pants, his flannel open down to mid-chest, revealing a dirty white T-shirt beneath. If it had been winter, he'd have worn a waffle-knit, long-john shirt instead. Orange Stihl suspenders over both shirts. Black steel-toed work boots. Grungy baseball cap to protect his bald spot from the sun. I could watch, in my mind, the cigarette break he'd taken an hour before, the lunch he'd eaten before that. Bologna or ham sandwich on white bread, pulled from that dented metal lunch pail, and the last of the coffee he'd brought with him that morning in his sage-green Stanley thermos. I could paint this for myself and feel sure it was true. But until I stood there in the field,

I'd been unable to imagine what he saw. It seemed important I find out, important to complete my dream of his death.

We went there around four in the afternoon because it was about the same time he died. Afternoon sun made the yellow field buttery. It gave off warmth. Green touched every edge of the field. Lush where the forest met the cultivated land and, from there, evergreens climbed. I thought of Packwood, a few hundred miles north of where I stood, of Mount Rainier, where I'd caught the steelhead whose descendants might be making their way home, climbing that mountain, at the same moment. Beyond the rising trees was wide sky, clouds making their slow way, changing shapes as they drifted. So many good people die in sterile hospitals, in sick-smelling beds or in bloody conflict. Loyd died working in fresh mountain air, on a bed of soft golden light, surrounded by living hills and a sky blue with summer. A view that makes the promise of heaven feel inevitable.

Once I'd stood in Loyd's place, I could complete my image of his death. I could see his body tense up as he stood tall and understood something was wrong. I knew he lifted his eyes and I knew why. If this was it, he wanted to see the trees. I thought of his voice on the phone, calling to tell me he loved me in case Y2K really happened, and I knew he thought of me and of Jesse when he lifted his eyes to the tree line and died. I could feel his heart stop, the blood slowing in his veins. Oxygen stopped feeding his muscles, his knees bent, and he gave in to the same genetic fate as his mother. I can see him fold down to the ground and lie in that field that looked like it might grace the cover of a *Watchtower* pamphlet.

Loyd's mother had only ever been a story to me. Now Loyd would only ever be a story to my daughter. I worry over this every day—will I only ever be a story to my grandchildren? Will sudden, early death be another unwanted inheritance from Loyd?

I wanted to see Loyd's body. Linda said I should forget about it, that it was better to remember him when he was alive. But she'd just been with him a few days before and I hadn't seen him in two years. And I think I needed proof. Somewhere in my mind, this idea still existed that the whole thing could be some bizarre mistake. Like I could go back to my family, changing diapers and scheduling play dates, and still have a dad out there in the world. The possibility of reunion.

Jesse understood why I wanted to see our dad, but he didn't need to himself. Uncle Papa was in Camas Valley by then and he felt the same way. Nobody else wanted to see Loyd's body. Jesse and Uncle Papa drove me to the funeral home in Winston and waited for me in the lobby. We'd called ahead so the funeral director was expecting us. We didn't pay for a viewing but he was nice about it. I think he could tell we didn't have much money. He'd pulled Loyd out of the icebox for me and set him up in a quiet room. It was tastefully decorated, beige and mauve, with art that could suit any religion. A trio of framed pictures of trees on one wall, a windswept landscape painting on another, silk floral arrangements on every table. It was a room that would've made Loyd feel out of place. He was out of place. I knew this was what Linda meant, when she'd pushed me to keep it simple. But nothing about my connection to Loyd was simple.

He was naked on a gurney, with a crisp white sheet pulled tight up his whole body, folded with a straight edge at his collarbones. I couldn't see his arms or his hands. I wanted to touch his hands. He'd gained a little weight since I saw him last. Linda told us that he'd been feeling sick the past few months. He was pretty sure it was something bad so he tried to see a doctor in Roseburg but was turned away because he didn't have insurance. He even felt bad enough to apply for the Oregon Health Plan but he was denied. According to the state, there was no reason a forty-eight-year-old man couldn't get a job with health insurance. Sitting there beside him, I tried to feel angry about that. But mostly I was just sad.

He was really clean, which felt like a violation. I couldn't smell pine or gasoline or cigarette smoke. Only floral bleach. I set my hand on his chest and it sent a vision up my arm. An image I only knew from Loyd, of the day he saved me from drowning. I saw him jumping in after my lifeless body, floating face down in tropical blue. His hunched back as he leaned over me in the dirt and pushed on my little chest. Now I could understand the miracle of that story. How a body without life can suddenly draw breath again. My hand on his chest pushed a little, once, twice, like he'd done for me. I didn't think I could bring him back or any-thing. He'd been dead three days already. It was an involuntary gesture. Acknowledging a gift he'd given because what's the use of holding on to all the injuries?

There was no more breath for Loyd, just cold seeping up from his body, through the sheet, into my hand. I was alone with him and that felt sort of precious. I touched his face. It was so stiff. When we were kids, he'd remove his false teeth so Jesse and I could play with his cheeks like Silly Putty. Now I ran my thumbs over his stone eyebrows the same way I did for my chil-dren, to help them fall asleep.

It seemed like I should do something or say something or have an instinct I was missing. I had to resist the urge to leave, end the visit too soon. Take time, I thought, sit with him. I ran my hands down his arm to feel his hand through the sheet. I touched each shoulder, like I was per-forming a religious ritual. Each touch confirmed a part of him, this was Loyd, my dad, and he was dead. Last chance, I told myself, you'll never see him again. I sat for a while longer. Touched his hand again. Ran my hand along the top of the sheet, tucking him in. I did not kiss him.

Later, I'd wish I'd taken pictures. So I could always go back to look at this moment that only I knew. That's what it was like for me and Loyd. At least when I was younger, before Packwood. I was always trying to keep him, to prove he existed.

As long as I could remember, Loyd kept this poem hanging around, wherever he was living at the time. It was printed over a picture of the sea. Sandy beach, tame waves, mostly blue sky with a few seagulls flying in focus.

If you love something, set it free.

If it comes back to you, it is yours.

If not, it was never meant to be.

It's not literature or anything, but I still get a lump in my throat when I see that poem. I had the sense, even as a kid, that this was his parenting guide. That this little saying helped him justify his long absences. It sup-ported his natural tendency, to keep his distance from people he consid-ered precious because it was only a matter of time before he hurt them.

And there's the whole "if it comes back to you" part. Possibility. Always the possibility of reconnection.

I didn't know it yet, but I'd lose Linda when I lost Loyd. She was about to disappear. Growing up, I sometimes imagined she'd disintegrate. I could see her connecting fibers loosen their bonds. Today, I talk about Linda in the past tense because I don't know if she's still alive. My sense is she's not.

Years before Loyd died, Linda had breast cancer. She figured it out and went to the doctor. She had a mastectomy but didn't put much effort into follow-up care after that. I'm guessing she gave her health even less attention after Loyd was gone. Jesse and I bought her one of those prepaid cell phones and she used it to keep in touch for a while. Eventually, she did what they'd always done. She lost touch. I sent her a holiday card every year with pictures of my kids. Always sent general delivery to Camas Valley. I can't know if those pictures were tacked up on a trailer wall somewhere or tossed in the trash at the post office. I try to imagine how Linda looks today, if she's alive. I wonder if she's in touch with her daughters, or if she made peace with them before dying. I want that for them, and for her.

Loyd was always clear that he wanted to be cremated, his ashes spread to the wind. Said he didn't need to *take up no more space on this earth*. Jesse and I figured that was fine. We were used to not having access to our dad in life. Why should it be any different in death? But Uncle Papa wanted his *little Bro* to have a marker, someplace he could always come visit. Linda didn't want a grave. She felt the idea was a betrayal of Loyd's wishes. Uncle Papa and Linda had a longstanding pissing match over Loyd, for probably twenty years or so. They didn't much speak to each other so Jesse and I played go-between. She threw her hands up, said we should do whatever we wanted. Said she had no legal say anyway. I don't think this was true but she was feeling lost. I was firm that Linda's opinion be considered. She, more than anyone, had been Loyd's partner. Jesse and I had to make the decision. I tried to be funny about it.

Well, if I had a dime for every time my dad betrayed MY wishes, I'd be rich. Everyone laughed like they did when I was little and said something stupid.

Peacemakers to the end, Jesse and I decided to split Loyd in two. Looking back, I think this is appropriate since that's what he'd always done to us. Split us in two. We gave half to Linda so she could spread them if she wanted. I never did hear what Linda did with her half of Loyd. We buried our half in Noah Cemetery.

I can't overstate how well this cemetery fits Loyd. There were no green rolling lawns or carefully trimmed hedges. Noah Cemetery is a little wild. It climbs up a brown grassy hillside dotted with scrubby pines. Driving in, the dirt road sort of circles the cemetery, with a couple smaller branches out into the center. I remember a bare white oak standing in the middle, at least I think it was an oak. There aren't really clear boundaries. The cemetery just sort of runs into the surrounding landscape. I don't think there's a regular groundskeeper or irrigation. A friendly volunteer met us there. He told us a general area and we dug our own hole.

Jesse and I couldn't afford a headstone. We were both so grateful at the funeral home when Uncle Papa whipped out a stack of hundred-dollar bills and pulled out six of them to pay for the cremation. My house needed a new furnace and it's not like Loyd left anything behind but debt. Jesse and I figured we'd make Loyd a headstone. We got pretty much everything we needed from the Home Depot in Roseburg.

Jesse used cedar two-by-fours to build a form and we poured it full of cement. We smoothed it out, tried to class it up a bit. I hired a guy at a machine shop in The Dalles to make lettering. He used some laser machine to cut words from marine brass and put spikes on the backs so we could sink them into the cement as it cured. We kept it pretty simple, just Loyd's name, birthdate, date he passed. I couldn't get behind any of the usual gravestone descriptors, *beloved husband, devoted father.* So we went with the first line of his favorite poem in letters smaller than his name. Across the top, *If You Love Something*, and across the bottom, *Set It Free.*

When we went back to the funeral home to pick up Loyd's ashes, the funeral director gave them to Jesse in a cardboard box. No fancy urn with the basic cremation package. It was a rectangular column with a matte white exterior. Jesse passed the box to me while he drove. I held it on my

lap and every time Jesse took a corner, I'd hear Loyd shifting, bone frag-
ments knocking together, like stirring gravel. All that was left of my dad
fit in a box about the size of his upper arms in life. Arms that used to hold
me up to the sky, or wrap around me when we wrestled, just after Loyd
hollered out, *timber!*

We had ashes and a headstone. We figured we might as well have a service. Nothing fancy, but it felt right. Grandpa Herb flew in from Louisiana
and Mom drove down.

When we were going through Loyd's stuff with Linda, I'd noticed small
scraps of paper, neatly torn and tacked up on the wall above a makeshift
desk of cinderblocks and rough boards. Each note a had bible verse in
Loyd's handwriting, the neat version. There was a bible on the desk and
some Watchtower Society literature so I took that to mean he'd been studying again. I asked Linda about it and she said a Witness had come knocking at their shack door, which I thought was pretty brave. I guess Loyd
respected that, too, because he invited the guy in and started meeting with
him once a week or so. I think the guy's name was Steve. One thing about
Loyd, he made many Jehovah's Witnesses happy in his life. He was usually
open to being saved.

I asked around and it didn't take long to find Steve. He was an average
white guy, looked about twelve years old. But he was Loyd's most recent
religious guide so I asked him to say a few words at Loyd's graveside. There's
no newspaper in Camas Valley, or at least there wasn't back then. But the
volunteer fire department had a newsletter most folks read. I made a dona-
tion and they put in an announcement of Loyd's death and our graveside
gathering.

Some locals gathered with us when we buried our half of Loyd.
Grandpa was the most compelling figure to me that day. I could hardly
keep my eyes off him. He stood over the small, deep hole, his feet almost
touching the edge, his hands pushing deep into the pockets of his denim
overalls. His wide cowboy hat blocked his face from the sun. Grandpa had
lost his father when he was ten years old. He was the eldest, so he went
to work right away to help support his mom and siblings. He'd buried his

wife, my Grandma Billie, when she was only forty-two. Just a couple years before that, they'd buried an infant son. Here he was putting another son in the ground. Looking at him, I could see it all. Some people just carry their grief physically, in a way that makes it visible.

For most of his eulogy, Steve was kind of dry and inarticulate. There were some *you knows* and *ums*, but mostly his speech seemed to come straight out of a pamphlet. He was clearly uncomfortable with public speaking and leadership, but eager to spread the Good News. I was beginning to think this speech was about the only part of this whole ramshackle funeral that didn't fit Loyd. But near the end of his speech, Steve said something remarkable, something I will always treasure.

Scripture teaches us, Steve said, that a little flock of one hundred and forty-four thousand will join God in the governing of a new and perfect paradise. This little flock will sit at the right hand of God in heaven.

Now Steve had my attention. I mean, where could he possibly be going with this? Nobody here was going to kid themself that Loyd made it into this little flock. A hundred and forty-four thousand is not very many people. I'm pretty sure everyone standing there, at least those who hadn't tuned Steve out, wondered how he'd bring this back to Loyd. He went on.

But scripture also speaks of the other sheep, which shall graze in the meadows of the new and perfect earth. Loyd was hoping to be one of these other sheep.

Emphasis on the *other*.

Now, I had no idea at the time that this whole *other sheep* concept is common among Jehovah's Witnesses. I didn't know that it would be deeply familiar to most Witnesses, probably was familiar to Loyd. To me, it just sounded like Loyd. I thought this was a line Steve came up with for this particular situation. And like so many things about Loyd, it came to me at exactly the perfect moment.

Loyd didn't dare aspire to be included in the little flock. People like Loyd don't govern anything. Look at his life! We can't just let this guy fuck up God's new and perfect paradise. He's lucky if he achieves other sheep status. I loved it. I giggled a little. Out loud. I pulled myself together pretty fast but I admit I let some audible laughter erupt. What a gift.

I was standing in a rural cemetery above a grave my brother dug next to a homemade concrete headstone that looked a bit like a grade-school craft project. We were there to bury a man who'd flashed in and out of our lives like a trickster character, inevitable and impossible. A man who taught me that love means loss. A man who was half of me.

I looked at my brother, heartbroken over the father he'd always worked so hard to please. I saw Mom, crying for their history. I felt Linda's absence, once again. Lost without her compass, she'd decided not to attend this service that would bind Loyd to one spot forever. I could feel the sorrow coming off Uncle Papa and Aunt Rainy, incomplete without their *Bro*. And I saw my Grandpa, there to bury his son and add another grief to his stooping shoulders.

I was looking at a disjointed family, steeped in addiction, poverty, violence, misogyny, and dysfunction. But I was also looking at love, acceptance, creativity, and slow, plodding perseverance against terrible odds. I was looking at my own flock, a flock made entirely of *other* sheep.

We were never a people who belonged to the little flock. And maybe that wisdom is what I needed from Loyd all along. Maybe he'd been trying to teach it to me my entire life. Not that I couldn't forget my backwoods start, the homesteads and the trailers, but that I shouldn't want to. Maybe Loyd, despite his frantic migrations between joy and grief, anger and love, shared something worth learning. It had just taken me a long time to get it. *Ain't nothin' for it but time, sweetheart.*

That day, I discovered a new truth about my flock. I understood that I get to choose what I keep and what I leave behind. I might not live among them, but I can carry them with me. I can love them and embrace our connection. Most important, I lost the drive to earn my way into the little flock, which exists in this world in so many forms. Wherever I went, I'd always find my place among the other sheep. And I'm cool with that.

thank you

THERE ARE SO MANY THINGS I wish I could do better in this book. Getting this part wrong scares me the most.

It can be terrifying to put memory to the page. What I tell and what I leave out shape the story I call truth. I owe endless thanks to my mom and my brother. It gives me comfort that you two, who lived these pages with me, took the time to read and help me bring memory and truth as close together as possible.

Thanks to my teachers and mentors, who encouraged me when I had no courage. Perrin Kerns and Kim Stafford, I'm so grateful. Perrin, you once told me that teaching is a way of giving back to the world. You read my pages, answer every email, every text. Jay Ponteri, you were the first person to tell me this story would be a book someday. Bhanu Kapil, you found a piece of litter on the ground, a blue string, and tied it around my wrist. It stayed there for two months while I worked on this book. A reminder that trash can sometimes bring the joyful color I need. Bea Gates, your continued support nourishes. You told me poets write the best memoirs and it was nice to know I didn't need to try and write the best memoir. Keenan Norris, your insights improved this book in countless ways. I am grateful for your faith in this project. As a teacher and a writer, you give me much to aspire to.

Perrin Kerns, again. Truly, there aren't enough words.

Thanks to all my family, living and gone, at Klindt's Booksellers. Kristin Klindt, Joaquin Perez, and everyone I was lucky to stand behind the bookstore counter with. Love and thanks to Jenny, Muir, and KJ Cohen at Waucoma Bookstore, also family. And to the indie bookselling community in the PNBA and beyond—we are a lucky people.

Kurtis Lowe, how could I even list all you've done? Your confidence has meant so much. I owe you many dinners. And thanks to your mom, Pam.

Lydia K. Valentine, you made me go to a party and then left me there. But you also made us family. You read pages for me and call me on my shit. So glad I offered you a ride that day. Shay Murphy, there was a day I almost decided not to turn in the final manuscript. You told me to put my big girl pants on and get 'er done. Avie Stacy, thank you for texting me quotes from my own book as you read an early draft and for spooning me when I need it. When I fall apart, I know you'll bring a shovel and scrape me up off the ground.

Thanks to friends and colleagues who read pages or passages, answered my anxious questions, or just always checked in to see how the writing was going. Christine Foye, Colleen Conway Ramos, Laura Stanfill, Lori Russell, Emily Moser, Nicole Thompson, Sarah Keller, Jayce Tappert, Rob Kovacich, Leigh Hancock, Dylan McManus, and so many more—your help and hope kept me going.

Thanks to my students, who continue to teach me more than I teach them.

My gratitude to the amazing team at OSU Press. Thanks to Tom Booth, Kim Hogeland, Marty Brown, and Micki Reaman for all the guidance, support, and faith.

Tammy and Hunter Carroll, thank you for being early readers and beloved family. Rod, Ida, and Lynda Ontiveros. Because you say this is the best book ever written and you haven't even read it. Thank you for loving me like that.

Melissa, Ema, and Ela. You inspire me. Your stories are unfolding as I write this and you're in the hard part. But you're made of strong stuff. Manos.

Sol and Lillian, you are my favorite things about this world. You made me a mother. We have created one another. These stories shaped you before I thought to tell them to you. Someday, I may have to face myself in your books. I look forward to that and to everything you'll make. Voo.

Ronnie Rho you beautiful genius, thanks for bringing me back to the woods so long ago. I love the way you always find the beauty and the joy, even though I'm grumpy about it sometimes (ok, most of the time). Thank you for working through my incessant anxieties and revisions with me. You are my favorite reader.

I owe more thanks than there is space for. If you've touched these pages or this story, I'm grateful.

Author's Note: This is a work of memory and any mistakes are mine alone. Names may have been changed or omitted to protect the living.

Jesse, Loyd, and Tina, July 1976